A SEED IS ALL YOU NEED
TO BE HEALED

A SEED IS

ALL

YOU NEED

TO BE

HEALED

Mark G Nolan

DEDICATION

To my much loved daughter Emma,
and granddaughters Hallie, Heidi, and Honey.
I dedicate this book to you.
With all my heart I hope you meet with the Lord of love,
for you will never know what true love is without Jesus,
because He is love, He is God, and God is love.
Jesus didn't come to bring religion, rules
or to condemn us for our sins. He came to save you and me.
He loved you so much that He Came to die on the cross
to set us free from the power of sin and death,
and He rose again from the grave in victory and glory.
Put your trust in Him to save you. He will not turn you away.
For God so loved the world (you), that He gave His only begotten
Son, that whosoever believes in Him should not perish,
but have eternal life.
Don't reject Him along with this wicked world.
This world will perish and everything in it.
But love will last forever and will never fail.
My hope is that I will see you again in paradise.

Love always Dad, and Grandad. xxxx

CONTENTS

ACKNOWLEDGMENTS

I want to thank my answered prayer and wife, Ruth, wonder woman, for the endless hours she put into typing, and editing this book, and encouraging me to keep going when the chips were down, for praying with me and for me the many times I came under attack from spirits and men. I couldn't have done it without you. I'll love you forever.

To Jenny Halligan who again spent many hours reading and correcting my terrible English grammar, even whilst suffering with your very own sore eye condition. Thank you so much for the great encouragement you always give.

I am so grateful to you both, this was a team effort and your reward will be great in heaven. May the Lord richly bless you both for all the hard work you put in to this book, all my love Mark xxx

"For we cannot but speak the things which we have seen and heard"

Acts 4:20

INTRODUCTION

A CURE FOR ANY SICKNESS

There is a cure for every sickness on earth. There isn't a sickness that cannot be cured. There is hope for those who have lost hope, and there is a way where there seems to be no way, to overturn the negative diagnosis, to refuse to accept what man says and rather to believe God instead.

This book is a written testament of real life events that have taken place over a fifteen year period. My wife, Ruth, and I have seen the so-called impossible happen many times, right before our eyes. It almost became a weekly event at one stage. The secret to our faith is simple; we chose to believe what Jesus said. No more, no less.

Jesus said
   "They shall lay hands on the sick, and they shall recover."
(Mk 16:18, KJV)

We chose to believe it, and so it happened. Simple, if you can just accept it for what it is; the truth. Jesus is the way, the truth, and the life. He will never let you down... simply because it is impossible for Him to make a false statement or tell a lie.

He is the truth, and the personification of all truth. Therefore, He, Jesus, being the truth, cannot make a promise that couldn't be true or could possibly fail to come to pass. No one has ever, or will ever prove Jesus wrong. A few have tried and failed.

If you believe, you will receive, but if you doubt, you will get nowt! But, there can be some blockages that prevent that immense healing power being released. I am going to be sharing what I have learnt. I realise the complexity of this subject, so I have asked the Lord for some help. Here goes.

KNOWING THE TRUTH CAN SET US FREE

A blockage is something that prevents the power from God being released. The power is freely available to everyone, but not all have the knowledge that could set them free.

The Lord said,
"My people are destroyed for lack of knowledge."
(Hos 4:6, KJV)

If a lack of the right knowledge can destroy us, then by receiving the right knowledge and putting it into action, we can be healed and saved.

Jesus said, "So I say to you, ask, and it will be given to you;
Seek, and you will find; knock and it will be opened to you.
For everyone who asks receives, and he who seeks finds,
And to him who knocks it will be opened."
(Lk 11:9-10, NKJV)

Even if we only have the smallest amount of faith, we can still knock and Jesus will open unto us. There is healing power available to all who would only believe, and life eternal for those who choose to follow and obey Him.

There is a way to be healed from any disease known to man. A cure was made freely available to every person on this planet, by the death, burial and resurrection of Christ Jesus two thousand years ago. Jesus is the healer and the only Saviour, yet there are many people who are still totally unaware.

Purely through a lack of biblical knowledge, people are suffering needlessly and are dying every day. I believe with all my heart that there is hope for those who are sick, and for people who have spent all their money on doctors, medicines and various cures without success.

Over the last fifteen years, my wife and I have seen many people totally cured from diabetes, lung cancer, and prostate cancer to name a few. We have seen the supernatural power of God, from seeing a person raised from the dead, to witnessing people being delivered from demons.

We want you, the reader, to realise that these accounts were the Lords doings, not ours. He purposed all the events that have taken place and have been recorded in this book. He, the Lord Jesus, was the one performing all the healing miracles, and He is the one who receives all the glory.

My aim is to give hope to the hopeless and to those who have been told that nothing can be done for them. This may be the case naturally, but it certainly isn't the case supernaturally.

I say this, nothing is impossible for God, and that all things are possible for those who believe. The awesome power in a minute seed of faith can, does, and will move mountains, whatever your mountain is.

SEEING IS BELIEVING

The people of this world say that seeing is believing. But God says that believing is seeing. We can see the results of faith when we put it into action.

> For we walk by faith, and not by sight.
>
> (2 Cor 5:7, NKJV)

By nature, we all find it hard to believe in something we cannot see. A man or woman who enjoys sailing yachts, for instance, cannot see the wind in their sails, but they know that this invisible force will propel them along at a rapid rate of knots. Although the people sailing cannot see the wind, they still know that it's there. They put their total trust in the force that they cannot see, and put their faith in its power to propel them along.

Would anybody dream of telling a yachtsman that we don't believe there is such a thing as the wind? He would think you are completely mad because it's contrary to his experience. But when we try and witness to anybody about the supernatural, invisible power of God, they too look at you as if you have lost your marbles.

There are many other invisible forces that we all take for granted and accept as just the norm. We cannot see micro waves, but we can see and feel the heat that is generated from them. We cannot see the air that we breathe, but without it, we would die.

With the naked eye, we are unable to see atoms, but the force of an atom bomb can destroy a city in seconds. We can't see quantum particles, infrared and ultraviolet light, or even the gravity which holds us firmly to the earth's surface.

Where would we be without these invisible elements?

> For the invisible things of Him from the creation of the world are clearly seen, being understood by the things that are made, even His eternal power and Godhead; so that they are

without excuse.

(Rom 1:20, KJV)

But God has chosen the foolish things of the world to put to shame the wise.

(1 Cor 1:27, NKJV)

We think that because we cannot see something, it isn't there. Yet hear the words of Jesus after He appeared to His disciples after His resurrection.

Jesus said to him, "Thomas, because you have seen Me, you have believed. Blessed are those who have not seen, and yet believed."

(Jn 20:29, NKJV)

AUTHORS TESTIMONY

I was forty one, recently married to Ruth, and I was bleeding internally. Every time I went to the toilet, I noticed blood coming from my behind. Having lost an uncle through stomach cancer, I was convinced that the same was going to happen to me. Out of fear, I buried my head in the sand and hoped that the bleeding would stop. It didn't.

Over the weeks, I became weaker and weaker, until one day I couldn't walk up the stairs. My heart was pounding and fear began to consume me. I rang the NHS helpline, and a doctor was sent out immediately. He took one look at me and said that I needed to get to the hospital as I had lost so much blood. He was very calm, but I could see the fear in his eyes.

I began to panic. Not thinking straight, I grabbed my car keys and drove with my wife to the hospital four miles away. I realise now that by not waiting for an ambulance, not only did I endanger my own life by driving, but I could have collapsed at the wheel with my wife in the car too.

We arrived at the hospital A and E, my heart still thumping in my chest. The lady at the counter was asking for my details, unaware of the severity of my condition. She told me to walk around to the rear of the building, which I couldn't believe, but did anyway.

My wife supported me as we made our way to the other entrance, and I suddenly said to myself, "Where would I go if I were to die right now? Heaven or Hell?" An overwhelming fear came over me which made my heart beat even faster.

We finally found the entrance to the correct ward, but to our astonishment, security had locked all the doors to the hospital as it was late in the evening. I couldn't believe what was happening; I was dying at the closed doors of the hospital.

I saw a nurse outside having a cigarette and asked if she could help. It seemed as though time was standing still and everything was going in slow motion. I realised in my heart that if I died here, now, I would go to Hell. Past sins were flashing through my mind and the fear of God overwhelmed my thoughts as I stood there and prayed, "Jesus, save me!" I cried and repeated this prayer over and over whilst asking forgiveness again and again.

After what seemed like an eternity, finally the doors slid open, and we were able to get in. As we stepped into the corridor, a group of doctors and nurses were waiting and they shouted, "Are you Mark?" I wearily said "Yes", and in moments I was on a bed trolley travelling at vast speeds through different corridors.

I don't remember if I fell asleep or into unconsciousness, but I was woken by a nurse gently tapping my face, calling my name. As soon as I regained consciousness and realised I was still alive with tubes in both arms, I prayed again. "Jesus, if you save me, I will serve You the rest of my life."

I must have fallen asleep again; this same thing happened several times throughout the night, and every time I woke up I would pray, and was so glad to be alive. I woke the next day with the sun light beaming through the windows. It was Sunday morning.

The surgeon came and stood at the bottom of the bed.

"Good morning" he said, as he lifted my notes from a clip board.

"Good morning" I replied, knowing that something truly amazing had happened to me. I felt so alive and so grateful to God because I knew Jesus had saved me.

The surgeon asked me how I got here.

"I drove, then walked to the back of the hospital," I said. He took one look at me in astonishment, shaking his head in disbelief. "If my heart would have stopped, would you have been able to get it going again?" I asked. "No" he replied. "You didn't have enough blood to help it to pump."

Then he made a statement that I'll never forget. "I have never seen anyone vertical in all my life as a surgeon with such a low blood count." I knew by his puzzled expression that I should be dead in the morgue with a tag on my toe. But God heard my cry and saved me from certain death, and that was how I came to be born again. I was so overwhelmed that I was alive, but knew that I was also spiritually alive for the first time. I asked a nurse what day it was; she replied that it was Easter Sunday morning.

The magnitude of what had happened filled my heart with love and joy for the Lord that I had never experienced before. I wanted to thank Him so I went in my pyjamas to the chapel, not realizing that there was a service taking place. I had no shoes on my feet, and I didn't care. I was greeted with a few strange looks, but I was there to thank and praise God. Jesus had resurrected me from the dead on resurrection Sunday.

I knew it was a physical impossibility for me to still be breathing. I am so grateful to the Lord for giving me eternal life. I ask people if they have ever seen a miracle, and most will say no. I always reply, "You have now, you're looking at one."

Jesus died my death; He took my sin, and nailed it to a tree. He took my death and rose again. Praise be to the Lord and Saviour, for all eternity we will thank Him, for all eternity I will praise Him. All honour, all praise, and all glory belong to my Lord, my Healer.

THE WAY TO HEALING AND SALVATION

I love the account of the thief on the cross in Luke 23:33-43 and recommend that you read it through. What did the thief do to receive complete forgiveness for a life time of wilful sinning against a pure and Holy God? First, he knew he was deserving of his punishment, both on the cross, and in Hell.

> Then one of the criminals who were hanging blasphemed
> Him, saying, "If You are the Christ, save Yourself and us."
> But the other answering, rebuked him, saying, "Do you
> not even fear God, seeing you are under the same
> condemnation?
> And we indeed justly, for we receive the due reward for our
> deeds; but this Man has done nothing wrong."
> (Lk 23:39-41, NKJV)

This man wasn't self-righteous. He hadn't deluded himself into believing that he was a good person. It was evident to all that he was a thief after all, with the accusation hanging over his head declaring it to the world.

So what did the thief do to get saved, and be assured from Jesus of a place in Paradise? He feared God's wrath. He admitted what he was. He knew that Jesus was sinless, because he declared that, "this man has done nothing wrong." And more than this, the thief believed the accusation above the head of Jesus.

"THIS IS THE KING OF THE JEWS"

(Lk 23:38, NKJV)

Despite the fact that this King was being crucified amidst two criminals, the thief made a surprising confession of faith as they were dying together.

> Then he said to Jesus, "Lord, remember me when You come into Your Kingdom."

(Lk 23:42, NKJV)

He believed Jesus was a King and had a Kingdom, despite the appalling circumstances. In believing, he was able to put his life and his fate into the Saviour's hands, and he put his faith into action by asking Jesus a question. I know that this dear brother is now in Paradise with the Lord because he feared God, admitted his sin, believed on Jesus, and asked that he would remember him.

Dear reader, if you can do the same, you will be saved. Jesus died your death. He took your punishment. He rose again, so that by His stripes we are healed. The blockage for salvation and healing is sin. Sin is the cause of all suffering and death in this world. The cure for all sickness and death is the blood of Jesus, and is activated by faith in Him alone.

PART 1

A SEED IS ALL YOU NEED

TO BE HEALED

WHAT DOES THE BIBLE SAY ABOUT HEALING?

Bless The Lord, O my soul: And all that is within me, bless His Holy name.

Bless The Lord, O my soul, and forget not all His benefits: Who forgives all your iniquities; who heals all your diseases

(Ps 103:1-3, NKJV)

Jesus said, "Your faith has made you well."　　(Mk 10:52, NKJV)

"Your faith has saved you."　　(Lk 7:50, NKJV)

"Thy faith has made thee whole."　　(Matt 9:22, KJV)

So, how much faith do we need to be healed, saved, made well or made whole?

Jesus said,

"I say to you, if you have faith as a mustard seed, you will say to this mountain, 'Move from here to there,' and it will move."

(Matt 17:20, NKJV)

We can trust in what Jesus promised, knowing that He doesn't make false promises.

Jesus said,

"I am the way, the truth, and the life."

(Jn 14:6, KJV)

The Lord has proved Himself faithful to His word many times in my own personal experience. Many Christians may think, "If I only had more faith, then I could lay my hands on the sick and they would recover," as promised in Mark 16.

But the fact is, that the only qualification we need to be able to heal in Jesus' name, is to be a believer in Christ.

> These signs shall follow them that believe;
> In my name they shall cast out devils;
> They shall speak with new tongues;
> They shall take up serpents; and if they drink any
> Deadly thing, it shall not hurt them;
> They shall lay hands on the sick, and they shall recover.
>
> (Mk 16:17-18, KJV)

The only thing you have to be to lay your hands on the sick, is a believer in Christ. You do not have to be an evangelist, or a pastor. The only qualification is to believe. A Roman soldier came to Jesus on behalf of his sick servant, and said

> "Lord, speak the word only and my servant shall be healed."
>
> (Matt 8:8, KJV)

After a lengthy conversation, Jesus said,

> "Go your way; and as you have believed, so let it be done for you." And his servant was healed that same hour."
>
> (Matt 8:13, NKJV)

This Roman soldier wasn't a Jewish leader, or even a religious man. He had probably killed many men and done many wicked things that any Roman soldier was expected to do. But He believed that Jesus could heal.

He didn't feel worthy enough to allow Jesus into his house, but he believed. The Roman's sins didn't prevent the servant from being healed, and also we see that he came on behalf of one he loved, not for himself.

WHAT DOES THE BIBLE SAY ABOUT HEALING?

God invites you to plead your case

> Even I, am He who blots out your transgressions for My own sake; And I will not remember your sins.
> Put Me in remembrance;
> Let us contend together; State your case, that you may be acquitted.
>
> (Is 43:25-26, NKJV)

God's word brings health and life.

> My son, give attention to my words; Incline your ear to my sayings. Do not let them depart from your eyes; Keep them in the midst of your heart. For they are life to those who find them, and health to all their flesh.
>
> (Prov 4:20-22, NKJV)

Jesus bore your sins AND your sicknesses.

> But He was wounded for our transgressions, He was bruised for our iniquities; the chastisement for our peace was upon Him, and by His stripes we are healed.
>
> (Is 53:5, KJV)

> Who Himself bore our sins in His own body on the tree, that we, having died to sins, might live for righteousness; by whose stripes you were healed.
>
> (1 Pet 2:24, NKJV)

God's benefits include healing.

> Bless the LORD, O my soul; And all that is within me, bless His holy name!
> Bless the LORD, O my soul, And forget not all His benefits: Who forgives all your iniquities, Who heals all your diseases,
> Who redeems your life from destruction, Who crowns you with loving-kindness and tender mercies,
> Who satisfies your mouth with good things, So that your youth is renewed like the eagle's.
>
> (Ps 103:1-5, NKJV)

God will restore your health.

> 'For I will restore health to you and heal you of your wounds,' says the LORD, 'because they called you an outcast saying: "This is Zion; No one seeks her."'
>
> (Jer 30:17, NKJV)

It is God's will for you to be healed.

> And behold, a leper came and worshipped Him, saying, "Lord, if You are willing, You can make me clean." Then Jesus put out His hand and touched him, saying, "I am willing; be cleansed." Immediately his leprosy was cleansed."
>
> (Matt 8:2-3, NKJV)

The Spirit of Life is making your body alive.

> But if the Spirit of Him who raised Jesus from the dead dwells in you, He who raised Christ from the dead will also give life to your mortal bodies through His Spirit who dwells in you.
>
> (Rom 8:11, NKJV)

God wants you to live.

> You will live a long life. With long life I will satisfy him, and show him My salvation.

(Ps 91:16, NKJV)

I shall not die, but live, and declare the works of the LORD.
(Ps 118:17, NKJV)

You can take authority over the sickness in your body. As born again believers, we have been given all authority to lose people from afflictions and demons, and bind them in Jesus' name. When you speak this out in prayer, believe it has already happened.

> Assuredly, I say to you, whatever you bind on earth will be bound in heaven, and whatever you loose on earth will be loosed in heaven.
> (Matt 18:18, NKJV)

What you say will make a difference.

> So Jesus answered and said to them, "Have faith in God. "For assuredly, I say to you, whoever says to this mountain, 'Be removed and be cast into the sea,' and does not doubt in his heart, but believes that those things he says will be done, he will have whatever he says."
> (Mk 11:22-23, NKJV)

Believe, and you will receive.

> Therefore I say to you, whatever things you ask when you pray, believe that you receive them, and you will have them.
> (Mk 11:24, NKJV)

Have someone lay hands on you for healing.

> And these signs will follow those who believe: In My name they will cast out demons; they will speak with new tongues; they will take up serpents; and if they drink anything deadly, it will by no means hurt them; they will lay hands on the sick, and they will recover."
> (Mk 16:17-18, NKJV)

Be anointed with oil by a Christian who believes in healing.

> Is anyone among you sick? Let him call for the elders of the
> church, and let them pray over him, anointing him with oil in
> the name of the Lord. And the prayer of faith will save the sick,
> and the Lord will raise him up. And if he has committed sins,
> he will be forgiven.
>
> (Jas 5:14-15, NKJV)

Agree with someone for your healing

> Again I say to you that if two of you agree on earth
> concerning anything that they ask, it will be done for them by
> My Father in heaven.
>
> (Matt 18:19, NKJV)

Be confident in your prayers.

> Now this is the confidence that we have in Him, that if we
> ask anything according to His will, He hears us. And if we know
> that He hears us, whatever we ask, we know that we have the
> petitions that we have asked of Him."
>
> (1 Jn 5:14-15, NKJV)

God answers the prayers of those that keep His commandments.

> Beloved, if our heart does not condemn us, we have
> confidence toward God. And whatever we ask we receive from
> Him, because we keep His commandments and do those things
> that are pleasing in His sight.
>
> (1 Jn 3:21-22, NKJV)

Worship God.

> Now we know that God does not hear sinners; but if anyone
> is a worshiper of God and does His will, He hears him.
>
> (Jn 9:31, NKJV)

KEEPING YOR EYES ON JESUS

Jesus Christ never changes. What He did in the Bible, He will do for you today.

> Jesus Christ is the same yesterday, today, and forever.
> (Heb 13:8, NKJV)

The devil wants to kill you; God wants to heal you.

> The thief does not come except to steal, and to kill, and to destroy. I have come that they may have life, and that they may have it more abundantly.
> (Jn 10:10, NKJV)

You are redeemed from the curse.

> Christ has redeemed us from the curse of the law, having become a curse for us (for it is written, "Cursed is everyone who hangs on a tree"), that the blessing of Abraham might come upon the Gentiles in Christ Jesus, that we might receive the promise of the Spirit through faith.
> (Gal 3:13-14, NKJV)

You will not waiver in your faith.

> Let us hold fast the confession of our hope without wavering, for He who promised is faithful.
> (Heb 10:23, NKJV)

God's Word will not fail.

> Not a word failed of any good thing which the LORD had spoken to the house of Israel. All came to pass.
> (Josh 21:45, NKJV)

God's Word is healing.

> He sent His word and healed them, and delivered them from their destructions.
>
> (Ps 107:20, NKJV)

God is for you.

> For all the promises of God in Him are Yes, and in Him Amen, to the glory of God through us.
>
> (2 Cor 1:20, NKJV)

You can have confidence in God and His Word.

> Therefore do not cast away your confidence, which has great reward.
>
> (Heb 10:35, NKJV)

You can find strength in God and His Word

> Let the weak say, "I am strong."
>
> (Joel 3:10, NKJV)

God's highest wish is for you to be well.

> Beloved, I pray that you may prosper in all things and be in health, just as your soul prospers.
>
> (3 Jn 1:2, NKJV)

Fear is not of God. Rebuke it!

> For God has not given us a spirit of fear, but of power and of love and of a sound mind.
>
> (2 Tim 1:7, NKJV)

Cast down the thoughts and imaginations that don't line up with the Word of God.

> For the weapons of our warfare are not carnal but mighty in
> God for pulling down strongholds, casting down arguments
> and every high thing that exalts itself against the knowledge of
> God, bringing every thought into captivity to the obedience of
> Christ.
>
> (2 Cor 10:4-5, NKJV)

Be strong in the Lord's power. Put on His armour to fight for
healing.

> Finally, my brethren, be strong in the Lord and in the power
> of His might. Put on the whole armour of God that you may be
> able to stand against the wiles of the devil.
>
> For we do not wrestle against flesh and blood, but against
> principalities, against powers, against the rulers of the darkness
> of this age, against spiritual hosts of wickedness in the heavenly
> places.
>
> Therefore take up the whole armour of God that you
> may be able to withstand in the evil day, and having done all,
> to stand.
>
> Stand therefore, having girded your waist with truth,
> having put on the breastplate of righteousness, and having shod
> your feet with the preparation of the Gospel of peace;
>
> above all, taking the shield of faith with which you will be
> able to quench all the fiery darts of the wicked one.
>
> And take the helmet of salvation, and the sword of the Spirit,
> which is the word of God.
>
> (Eph 6:10-17, NKJV)

Give testimony of your healing.

> And they overcame him by the blood of the Lamb and by the
> word of their testimony, and they did not love their lives to the
> death.
>
> (Rev 12:11, NKJV)

ARE THE GIFTS OF HEALING FOR TODAY, IN OUR TIME?

As we read the Bible, it needs to be interpreted through the illumination of the Holy Spirit. Bible scriptures can often be misinterpreted, and it's possible to disannul, or take away the power that is contained in the word of God. An example of this is in 1 Corinthians 13:8-12

> Charity never fails, but whether there be prophesies, they
> shall fail, Whether there be tongues, they shall cease,
> Whether there be knowledge, it shall vanish away.
> For we know in part, and we prophesy in part.
> But when that which is perfect is come, then that which is part
> shall be done away with.
> For now we see through a glass, darkly, but then face to face.

There is an argument amongst some bible scholars who believe that the gifts of the Holy Spirit were done away with when the apostles died. But this teaching is false for many reasons.

Some people put their trust in a man because he has been to Bible College and obtained a P.H.D, and therefore he must know what he is talking about. Yet they fail to study the bible for themselves, or even come before The Lord in prayer, seeking His interpretation. We must keep in mind this warning.

> Cursed be the man that trusts in man, and makes flesh his
> arm, and whose heart departs from the LORD.

(Jer 17:5, NKJV)

We must always be sure to read the scriptures for ourselves and ask the Lord to reveal His truth to us. On looking at the list above from 1 Corinthians, at first glance it appears that some of the gifts have been done away with. But when we look closer, we can see that there is no suggestion that the gifts have ceased yet, and the gift of healing isn't even mentioned.

The apostle Paul is saying here that prophesies will fail, tongues will cease, and knowledge will vanish away, but they will only cease when perfection comes. What is perfection? The coming of Jesus Christ Himself. When He has come, then and only then will we have no need of the gifts mentioned. A prophet will not be needed to give a word from the Lord because the Lord Himself will be here. There will be no need for the gift of tongues and interpretation, because we will hear His voice and see Him face to face.

> These signs shall follow them that believe.
> In My name they shall cast out devils, they shall speak with
> new tongues;
> They shall take up serpents, and if they drink anything deadly
> it shall not hurt them. They shall lay their hands on the sick and
> they shall recover.
>
> (Mk 16:17-18, KJV)

Until perfection comes, the gifts remain. We can have confidence in the word of God.

I AND THE FATHER ARE ONE

Would it be too difficult for the same God who created the vast universe and the magnificent world we live in to repair a minor fault in the human body that He designed? The chief designer of the eyes surely knows how to repair them. Just imagine the awesome power Jesus demonstrated on Earth. God (Elohim)-(plural), Father, Son, and Holy Spirit created man together.

> And God (Elohim) said let us create man in (our) image.
> (Gen 1:26, KJV)

> So God created man in His own image, in the image of God created he him: male and female created he them.
> (Gen 1:27, KJV)

All things are possible for those who believe. In believing that Jesus is the all-powerful, Almighty God, I would say, is the key to a greater understanding of who Jesus is, because Jesus created all things.

> All things were created by Him and for Him.
> (Col 1:16, KJV)

When we know who Jesus is, then we can have confidence and know what He, as Almighty God, is capable of. He proved He was the creator when He created a pair of eyes for the man born blind.

When He had thus spoken, He spat on the ground, and made

clay of the spittle, and He anointed the eyes of the blind man with the clay, and said unto him, "Go, wash in the pool of Siloam." He went his way therefore, and washed, and came seeing.

(Jn 9:6-7, KJV)

As God Elohim, Father, Son and Holy Spirit, were involved in the creation of Adam, we see the whole God head was involved in the creation of a brand new pair of eyes for the blind man. Another example of a creation miracle by Jesus is when Peter had severed the ear of Malchus, when the soldiers came to arrest Jesus in the garden of Gethsemane.

And one of them smote the servant of the high priest, and cut off his right ear. And Jesus answered and said, "Suffer ye thus far." And He touched his ear and healed him.

(Lk 22:50-51, KJV)

From what we can see in this verse, Jesus didn't bend down to pick up the ear that had been chopped off; He simply touched Malchus and created a new one.

Jesus is the Father, the Son and the Holy Spirit, and therefore is the creator, the body maker, the saviour and healer, and the Holy Spirit is the Spirit of Jesus through which the power to heal is released through faith.

Let me go a little further in this amazing truth. I received this revelation one evening whilst visiting a Pakistani Christian worship and praise meeting with my wife. When the music had stopped, I was asked to share a word, and turned to the passage in John 3:13, when Jesus said

No man has ascended up to heaven, but he that came down from heaven, the son of man (Jesus) which (is) (in) (heaven).

So I asked, "How can Jesus be on earth and in Heaven at the same time?" The answer is, because He, Jesus, is Almighty God, connected through the Holy Spirit.

God Almighty became a man in the form of Yahoshua (Jesus) to put sinful flesh to death and make a way for salvation, healing, and redemption for those who would not only believe in Him, but would follow Him and do His will.

WAS GOD ON THE CROSS?

I felt it necessary to examine one more passage of scripture, not only to prove that Jesus is God Almighty, but to realise in a deeper way what God has done for us all.

This astonishing passage relating to just who Jesus was and is, can be found in the book of Zechariah. To get the true context of what is written, I thought it best to look at who it is that is speaking in this chapter that we shall be looking at.

Obviously it is being written by Zechariah the Prophet, but I am in no doubt that it is being dictated by God himself, through the Holy Spirit.

> The burden of the word of the Lord for Israel say's the Lord,
> *(This is almighty God speaking)*
> which stretches out the heavens, and that forms the spirit of
> man within him.
>
> (Zech 12: 1, NKJV)

Then as we progress through the chapter we come to one of the most astonishing passages in the whole bible.

> And I will pour upon the house of David, and upon the
> inhabitants of Jerusalem, the spirit of grace and of supplications:
> *(Please note, this is God almighty speaking.)*
> and they shall look upon me whom they have pierced,
> *(Who was pierced? God almighty.)*
> And they shall mourn for him, as one mourns for his only son,
> and shall be in bitterness for him, as one that is in bitterness for
> his firstborn.
>
> (Zech 12:10, NKJV)

Please note the whole Trinity is in this passage. God the father, God the Holy Spirit, and God the son. There are a lot of cults out there who minimize Jesus to being the mere son of God, or even an angel, and fail to see that Jesus is God Himself.

So, if Jesus is God, why did He say that the Father was greater than He?

> If you loved me, ye would rejoice, because I said, I go unto
> the Father: for my Father is greater than I.
>
> (Jn 14:28, KJV)

Jesus said that the Father was greater than He, not because Jesus is not God, but because Jesus was also a man, and as a man, he was in a lower position.

> But we see Jesus, who was made a little lower than the angels
> for the suffering of death.
>
> (Heb 2:9, KJV)

Let this mind be in you, which was also in Christ Jesus, Who being in the form of God thought it not robbery to be equal with God: but made Himself of no reputation and took upon Himself the form of a servant, and was made in the likeness of Men.

(Phil 2:5-7, KJV)

Jesus has two natures: divine and human. Jesus was not denying that He was God. He was merely acknowledging the fact that He was also a man. Jesus is both God and man. As a man, He was in a lesser position than the Father because He had added to Himself human nature.

For in Him dwells all the fullness of the Godhead bodily.

(Col 2:9, NKJV)

He was made under the Law

But when the fullness of the time was come, God sent forth His Son, made of a woman, made under the law.

(Gal 4:4, NKJV)

He became a man to die for people.

Moreover, brethren, I declare unto you the Gospel which I preached unto you, which also you have received, and wherein you stand; By which also you are saved, if you keep in memory what I have preached unto you, unless you have believed in vain. For I delivered unto you first of all that which I also received, how that Christ died for our sins according to the scriptures; and that He was buried, and that He rose again the third day according to the scriptures.

(1 Cor 15:1-4, KJV)

This is the full Gospel of Jesus Christ. Jesus wasn't denying that He was God, He was simple acknowledging that He was also a man, and as a man, He was subject to the laws of God so that He might redeem those who were under the law, namely sinners.

ALL AUTHORITY

Behold, I give unto you power to tread on serpents and
scorpions, and over all the power of the enemy, and nothing
shall by any means hurt you.

(Lk 10:19, NKJV)

The word for "power" used here, in the Greek translates more
accurately as "authority." In other words, Jesus is not saying, "I give
you power over the devils power." He is saying "I give you authority
over all the power of the devil." For example, there might be an
enormous army coming against you, but if you have all authority
over that army, irrespective of its size and power, then that army is
subject to your authority, which renders it powerless.

Like a Sergeant Major on the parade ground, he commands his
soldiers. He doesn't request their cooperation, just gives orders. The
Roman centurion who came to Jesus said,

For I am a man under authority, having soldiers under me:
and I say to this man, 'go', and he goes; and to another, 'come',
and he comes; and to my servant, 'do this,' and he does it.

(Matt 8:9, NKJV)

The Roman soldier knew Jesus was a man of authority who could
command demons and sicknesses to leave. That's why the centurion
said to Jesus,

> Lord I am not worthy, that you should come under my roof:
> but speak the word only, and my servant shall be healed.
>
> (Matt 8:8, NKJV)

> When Jesus heard it, He marvelled, and said to those who
> followed, "Assuredly I say to you, I have not found such great
> faith, not even in Israel!"
>
> (Matt 8:10, NKJV)

Notice here that the centurion wasn't even coming for himself; he was coming to Jesus out of love for his servant. It was his faith in Christ which resulted in the centurion being saved. As is written,

> And he believed in the Lord; and he counted it to him for
> righteousness.
>
> (Gen 15:6, KJV)

If we have been born of the Spirit, then we have been given the badge of authority to command spirits to leave a body in Jesus' name. The same authority that the Heavenly Father gave to the Son has now been given to us. Jesus commanded with all authority. For example:

> Rise, take up your bed and walk. (Jn 5:8. NKJV)

> And He said to him,
> "Go wash in the pool of Siloam." (Jn 9:7, NKJV)

> But go and show yourself to the priest. (Lk 5:14, NKJV)

> Be quiet, and come out of him! (Lk 4:35, NKJV)

> Nevertheless do not rejoice in this, that the spirits are subject to you, but rather because your names are written in heaven.
>
> (Lk 10:20, NKJV)

A man himself has no power, but when he puts on his uniform, it then indicates who and what he has become. He swears an oath and he's declared to be an officer of the law when he is given the badge of authority. That badge not only proclaims who he is, but the power and authority that he has been given. The same applies to all born again Christians.

When we are born again, we are then empowered from within by the Holy Spirit for His Majesty's service. When we put on Christ, we are given His badge of authority, and we become ambassadors for Christ. This anointing power is given to us by the Lord, and we can declare

> The Spirit of The Lord is upon Me, because He has anointed Me to preach the Gospel to the poor; He has sent Me to heal the broken hearted, to proclaim liberty to the captives and recovery of sight to the blind, to set at liberty those who are oppressed; To preach the acceptable year of the Lord."
>
> (Lk 4:18-19, NKJV)

I CAN DO ALL THINGS THROUGH CHRIST

If you possess the Holy Spirit, and the Holy Spirit resides in your body, then your body has become the temple of the Living God. The power that spoke the universe into being indwells in you. The amazing thing that I find totally mind blowing, is the fact that this power is given to us and released through Jesus' name. You then have all the power and authority of the Godhead, Father, Son and Holy Spirit, that can be activated by a mustard seed of faith.

Nothing is impossible for God. We can do all things through Christ who strengthens us, for we have been given all authority over the powers of darkness. As the demons trembled when they saw Jesus approaching, they should tremble when they see the Holy Spirit in us.

The problem is that most Christians are unaware of the awesome power that is available to them, through the almighty, name of Jesus. If you have been born of the Spirit, then you have the power to cast out all spirits of infirmity in Jesus' name.

> You are of God, little children, and have overcome them:
> Because, greater is He that is in you, than he that is in the world.
> (1 Jn 4:4, NKJV)

They cannot refuse to go. We, who are born of the Spirit, can do everything Jesus did. In fact the Lord declared that His servants would do mightier works than He had done. This declaration of Christ still remains today, because He is the same, yesterday, today and forever.

A note to think about here is that even the unsaved have the power to cast out devils and heal in Jesus' name. For instance,

> Many will say to Me in that day, 'Lord, Lord, have we not
> prophesied in Your name, cast out demons in Your name,
> and done many wonders in Your name?' And then I will declare
> to them, 'I never knew you; depart from Me, you who practise
> lawlessness.'
> (Matt 7:22-23, NKJV)

The astonishing fact in this declaration by Jesus is that even the unsaved, who don't have the Holy Spirit are able to prophesy, cast out devils and do wonderful works, which I believe include healing. This proves to me that the power is not in the people, but lies in the awesome power of the name of Jesus.

YOUR FAITH HAS MADE YOU WHOLE

There are millions of people who are seeking a cure for their disease or infirmity. I have no doubt they have tried many so called different remedies that have failed. But if people are just seeking to heal their bodies, they are missing the point as they can be made completely whole, because we are triune beings, created in God's image, body, soul and spirit.

There are three parts to us, not just one. To receive healing on the body would only be superficial and temporary. Would someone only seek a temporary solution when there is a permanent one now available? Why would anyone want to heal only the body, and leave the soul and spirit still in sickness?

If all you are looking for is healing for your body, God may well grant healing for you through His awesome compassion and love. After all, those who are suffering in this world are seeking a temporary relief from pain, suffering and discomfort, because ultimately death will follow us all.

Healing the body would be as Jesus said, only washing the outside of the cup.

"Woe unto you, scribes and Pharisees, hypocrites! For you make clean the outside of the cup and the dish, but within they are full of extortion and excess. You blind Pharisees, cleanse first that which is within the cup and the dish, that the outside of them may be clean also."

(Matt 23:25-26, NKJV)

Before making a cup of tea or coffee, we wouldn't just clean the outside of the cup and leave the inside stained with tea and coffee. Just imagine never washing the cup, we would probably get a disease and die from drinking from a dirty cup continually. Like most people, the Pharisees in this passage look clean and holy on the outside, but as Jesus pointed out that inside they are full of dead men's bones, and all hypocrisy.

They were only concerned with the external appearance of how they looked to man on the outside, but God looks at the inside.

> Woe to you, scribes and Pharisees, hypocrites!
> For you are like white washed tombs which indeed appear beautiful outwardly, but inside are full of dead men's bones and all uncleanness.
> Even so you also outwardly appear righteous men, but inside you are full of hypocrisy and lawlessness.

(Matt 23:27-28, NKJV)

After this verbal lashing of truth, the Pharisees were even more determined to kill Jesus. There is no good thing in the flesh, this may come as a major revelation to those people who think they are righteous before God by the good deeds they have done.

> For I know that in me, that is in my flesh, dwells no good thing.

(Rom 7:18, NKJV)

Therefore, there is nothing we can do externally to cleanse the soul internally. You see, nothing that we can do on the outside, good deeds, church attendance, donations to the poor, can ever make us clean. Likewise, you may receive bodily healing, but you could still be lost for eternity and separated from God, because the inside hasn't been cleansed or made whole. External works are only temporal.

HEALED IN SOUL, HEALED IN BODY

A direct sign that a person has had their sins forgiven is the manifestation of physical healing. When the spirit of affliction is driven out of the body by the Holy Spirit, the soul is cleansed and the person is made whole by their faith in Jesus. This has nothing to do with what they have done outwardly, but is a result of what the Holy Spirit has done inwardly.

The person is healed completely, body, soul and spirit. We can see a perfect example of this in Mark 2. I realise I may be getting into hot water with some theologians, but please try and bear with me.
Jesus said

> "But that you may know that the Son of Man has power on earth to forgive sins." He said to the paralytic, "I say to you, arise, take up your bed, and go to your house."
>
> (Mk 2:10-11, NKJV)

> Which is easier, to say to the paralytic, 'Your sins are forgiven you,' or to say, 'Arise, take up your bed, and walk?'
>
> (Mk 2:9, NKJV)

Jesus is saying that it's as easy to forgive the man's sins as it is to heal his body. In other words, Jesus is saying, "That you may know that I have power to release this man from his sins, the outward sign that this man's sins have been forgiven, shall be that the spirit of infirmity has gone and the regenerating power of the Holy Spirit, eternal life and health has entered into the soul and the spirit, releasing him from the captivity of the soul, which resulted in releasing this man from his physical condition."

Everyone that came to Jesus and asked for healing was healed, but I have no doubt that God does occasionally leave some infirmities in a saint's body to show His glory through our weakness. Moses stammered, and St Paul had either physical ailments or poor eyesight, or a speech impediment. We are not exactly sure but I think this next scripture sums it up.

> And He said to me, "My grace is sufficient for you, for My strength is made perfect in weakness." Therefore most gladly I will rather boast in my infirmities, that the power of Christ may rest upon me.
> Therefore I take pleasure in infirmities, in reproaches, in needs, in persecutions, in distresses, for Christ's sake.
> For when I am weak, then I am strong.
> (2 Cor 12:9-10, NKJV)

In conclusion, I personally wouldn't want just temporary physical healing when I could be given the whole complete regeneration of body, soul and spirit, and in the world to come pleasures for ever more in the Kingdom of God with my love, my life and my Saviour, Jesus.

So in conclusion, we need to spend time as a living sacrifice with the Lord when praying for ourselves and others. We need to accept that God hears our prayers, and then we ought to expect Him to do what He said He would do, when He hears our prayers of faith. God cannot and will not fail to act.

When we order the shopping online, we know that it has been paid for, is being delivered, and is on the way. We don't doubt that it is going to be delivered, we just expecting it to arrive. It is the same principle with God. We put our petition in; it has been paid in full by the blood of Christ, and is on the way. A thankful heart is a happy heart, is a receiving heart.

> He is a rewarder of them that diligently seek Him.
>
> (Heb 11:6, KJV)

SPEAKING THE WORD OUT LOUD

People receive faith by hearing the word of God being spoken out loud. When they receive faith, then and only then are they ready to receive healing.

Jesus went from village to village preaching the kingdom of God and repentance, and baptism for the remission of sins. Their faith in Jesus healed, saved and delivered them. The word has not lost its power, because Jesus is not in time, space or matter, we are. But He is omnipresent, all knowing and all seeing.

> A very present help in trouble.
>
> (Ps 46:1, KJV)

In some religions, their god is a far off, aloof, unapproachable, even a mystical figure, who is too holy to be present with a mere mortal. But that is not Jesus. Jesus came to heal the sin disease that separated us from His Father, so we can be back in a loving fellowship with Him.

By preaching the word to the sick, faith in Christ comes, and then the healing follows. It sounds simple doesn't it? That's because it is. When we speak the word, we come into agreement with the power in it. After all, the world was made by the word being spoken. Speak it out. Shout it from the rooftops.

ANOINTING WITH OIL

Is any among you afflicted?
(This word afflicted should read, as in the Greek interlinear, suffering hardships)
Let him pray. Is any merry? Let him sing psalms.
Is any sick among you? Let him call for the elders of the church; and let them pray over him, anointing him with oil in the name of the Lord.
And the prayer of faith shall save the sick, and the Lord shall raise him up; and if he have committed sins, they shall be forgiven him.
Confess your faults one to another, and pray one for another, that ye may be healed. The effectual fervent prayer of a righteous man availeth much.

(Jas 5:13-16, KJV)

And they cast out many devils, and anointed with oil many that were sick, and healed them.

(Mk 6:13, KJV)

There are several commands in the bible for the use of olive oil. These are found in Leviticus 2:15, 6:15, 1 Kings 17:12, psalm 23:5, 141:5, Zechariah 4:12, Exodus 29:7.

There are occasions in the bible where perfume was mixed with holy anointing oil.

> And you shall make from these a holy anointing oil, an ointment compounded according to the art of a perfumer. It shall be a holy anointing oil.
>
> (Ex 30:25, NKJV)

It was also mixed in the temple with spices.

> And some of the sons of the priests made the ointment of the spices.
>
> (1 Chron 9:30, NKJV)

I personally believe that only olive oil was used to pray over the sick. If anyone knows differently, please let me know. Because olive oil was used in the temple, I believe it has a special significance. Firstly, Israel is referred to as the olive branch; it was used in the Holy of Holies to light the lamps, being symbolic of Jesus as being the light of the world. Jesus was also being crushed in the garden of Gethsemane, meaning oil press.

LAYING ON OF HANDS

In the New Testament, there were two main reasons for the laying on of hands. The first one was for the receiving of the Holy Spirit, or what some call the Baptism of the Holy Spirit. This is found in Acts 8:14-19.

If you have not received the baptism of the Holy Spirit then you are not saved. It is only through receiving new birth by the Holy Spirit that you can say that you have become a child of God and are saved. Sadly there are many that attend church and do churchy things but have never been born of the Holy Spirit.

Jesus said
"Except a man be born of water and of Spirit, he cannot enter the kingdom of God."

(Jn 3:3, KJV)

The laying on of hands was to receive the Holy Spirit. The apostles would lay their hands on new believers who had already been baptised in water, to receive the Holy Spirit. This was the fulfilment of the promise spoken of by Peter in Acts 2:39.

The laying on of hands was to firstly receive eternal life, divine healing and salvation. We also receive power.

But you shall receive power, after the Holy Spirit has come upon you: And you shall be my witnesses unto me both in Jerusalem and in all Judaea, and the uttermost part of the earth.

(Acts 1:8, NKJV)

The laying on of hands was also for imparting spiritual gifts, and equipping the saints for spiritual warfare and missionary work in proclaiming the Gospel with power, plus appointing and anointing pastors, deacons and elders, for healing the sick with signs following the preaching of the word.

Go into all the world, and preach the Gospel to every creature. He who believes and is baptised shall be saved; but he who does not believe shall be condemned.

And these signs shall follow those who believe;
In My name they will cast out demons; they will speak with

new tongues; they will take up serpents; and if they drink
anything deadly, it will by no means hurt them;
They will lay hands on the sick, and they will recover.

(Mk 16:17-18, NKJV)

When I am praying with someone for their healing, once I have read the word of God to them, I ask if they are ready to be healed. If they say, not just yet, then I carry on reading the word to them until they receive the supernatural impartation of faith from God. Then and only then, will I anoint them with oil on the forehead in the name of the Father, the Son, and the Holy Spirit, and then lay hands on their head praying in Jesus' name.

Is any sick among you? Let him call for the elders of the
church; and let them pray over him, anointing him with oil in
the name of the Lord.

(Jas 5:14, KJV)

When you know that a person has faith to be healed, then you can lay hands on them, not before. Remember, when laying hands on someone, you must be gentle, like Jesus.

There are many examples found in the bible for the laying on of hands.

And He took them up in His arms, laid His hands on them,
and blessed them.

(Mk 10:16, NKJV)

My little daughter lies at the point of death: Come and lay

Your hands on her, that she may be healed, and she will live.

(Mk 5:23, NKJV)

When the sun was setting, all those who had any that were sick with various diseases brought them to Him; and He laid His hands on every one of them and healed them.

(Lk 4:40, NKJV)

Then they laid hands on them, and they received the Holy Spirit.

(Acts 8:17, NKJV)

Just a note, I always felt it was so important to pray over the sick using my right hand, and on reading this scripture I've just found out why.

I would like to point out that there are some self appointed pastors who look the part, talk the part and can even preach the part, but they are not anointed for the office that they've taken up. I once heard an evangelist saying that some of these self appointed pastors are mainly failed business men, who don't want to give up the suit. Therefore I have seen something that breaks my heart; many go for healing to the pastor and are never healed.

My advice would be to check out a few Pentecostal churches and ask the members of the congregation whether anybody gets healed in their church. That is a sure indication of whether the pastor is God appointed or self appointed.

RAVENOUS WOLVES IN SHEEP'S CLOTHING

There are many false evangelists out there who are just money making charlatans, like Benny Hinn, Kenneth Copeland, Rodney

Howard Brown and others. Nobody ever got healed through Benny Hinn, not one. They look like the sheep, and smell like the sheep, and speak all manner of flattering words to have men in admiration, but are inwardly ravenous wolves. Stay away from them and anybody who is asking for money in exchange for receiving answered prayer. Jesus said

> And as you go, preach, saying, "The kingdom of Heaven is at hand." Heal the sick, cleanse the lepers, raise the dead, cast out devils: Freely you have received, freely give.
>
> (Matt 10:8, NKJV)

A real man of God would never ask for money in order for you to receive your healing. A typical salesman like phrase would go something like this, "When you sow into this ministry, you will receive a larger amount back in return from the Lord." This is false.

I have also seen people who have been overwhelmed by the power of God and have gone down under the anointing, but I have also seen and experienced myself, that people have tried to physically push someone over. The best way to find out whether a particular ministry is kosher or not is to ask the Holy Spirit, but don't throw the baby out with the bath water.

> Beloved, believe not every spirit, but try the spirits whether they are of God: because many false prophets are gone out into the world.
>
> (1 Jn 4:4, KJV)

Over the years, I have seen some pastors shouting and literally pressing down on someone's head whilst shaking it violently. These poor people, if they didn't need an aspirin when they came forward for healing, they will certainly need one afterward.

There is no need for this sort of behaviour. Remember, Jesus doesn't need you to heal anyone. You are just an instrument of His grace. Always pray through His name.

From personal experience, I would stay away from the Assemblies of God, and from anybody who has been involved in the Toronto so-called blessing. In fact, I would stay away from anyone who wears a white suit and exalts himself on posters instead of exalting Jesus.

Jesus warned that many would come in his name to deceive many. Some people will say, who are you to judge other people? So, I want to make this clear, judgement starts first in the house of God, and we are warned in scripture to watch out for false evangelists, pastors and teachers, and to expose them, warning the sheep.

> Beware of false prophets, which come to you in sheep's clothing, but inwardly they are ravening wolves.
>
> (Matt 7:15, KJV)

Why else would Jesus warn us if it were not so?

ADDITIONAL EXAMPLES OF HEALING METHODS

CONFESSING SIN

> Confess your faults one to another, and pray one for another, that ye may be healed.
> The effectual fervent prayer of a righteous man availeth much.
>
> (Jas 5:16, KJV)

DELIVERANCE

When the evening was come, they brought unto Him many that were possessed with devils: and He cast out the spirits with His word, and healed all that were sick.

(Matt 8:16, KJV)

FAITH

For verily I say unto you, that whosoever shall say unto this mountain, be thou removed, and be cast into the sea; and shall not doubt in his heart, but shall believe that those things which he says shall come to pass; he shall have whatsoever he saith.

(Mk 11:23, KJV)

Notice here the focus on speech;

Whatsoever he *says*
But shall believe that those things which he *says*
He shall have whatsoever he *says*

It's no good just having faith. We need to audibly command the mountain of sickness to leave in Jesus' name, believing that it will come to pass.

VIRTUE OF TOUCH

For she said, "If I may touch but His clothes, I shall be whole. And straightway the fountain of her blood was dried up: and she felt in her body that she was healed of that plague.

(Mk 5:29-30, KJV)

PRAYER

And all things, whatsoever you shall ask in prayer, believing, ye shall receive.

(Matt 21:22, KJV)

PRESENCE OF GOD

And it came to pass on the certain day, as He was teaching, that the Pharisees and doctors of the law sitting by, which were come out of every town of Galilee and Judea, and Jerusalem: and the power of the Lord was present to heal them.

(Lk 5:17, KJV)

THE GIFT OF HEALING

To another faith by the same Spirit; to another the gift of healing by the same Spirit.

(1 Cor 12:9, KJV)

THE WORD OF GOD

He sent His word, and healed them, and delivered them from their destructions. O that men would praise The Lord for His goodness, and His wonderful works to the children of men.

And let them sacrifice the sacrifices of thanksgiving, and declare His works with rejoicing.

(Ps 107:20-22, KJV)

CLOTHING

So that from His body were brought unto the sick

handkerchiefs and aprons, and the diseases departed from them, and the evil spirits went out of them.

(Acts 19:12, KJV)

FASTING

Is not this the fast that I have chosen? To lose the bands of wickedness, to undo the heavy burdens, and to let the oppressed go free, and that ye break every yoke?

Is it not to deal thy bread to the hungry and that thou bring the poor that are cast out to thy house?

When thou seest the naked, that thou cover him: and that thou hide not thyself from thine own flesh?

Then shall thy light break forth as the morning, and thy health shall spring forth speedily: and thy righteousness shall go forth before you; the glory of the Lord shall be thy reward.

(Is 58:6-8, KJV)

And He said unto them, "This kind can come forth by nothing, but by prayer and fasting."

(Mk 9:29, KJV)

A SEED IS ALL YOU NEED TO BE HEALED

PROCLAIMING THE WORD THAT HEALS

RENEWING THE MIND

When we read the word of God, we begin to renew our minds. We go from the natural, carnal mind, and start to understand the supernatural mind of God. In fact, when we are born-again we are given the mind of Christ.

As the words of Christ are recorded for us to meditate on, and speak aloud, we become more spiritual and less carnal. Our faith increases and we begin to realise the potential power that is available to all who have but the smallest of faith.

The word of God will accomplish what it will, and is not based on the size of your faith. It is based on the power of the spoken word of God. So many Christian could pray over the sick for healing, but they don't believe that they have enough faith to see results. They are relying on their own strength instead of the infallible word of God.

If they had enough faith to get saved, then they have more than enough faith to put into action for healing. We have all the faith we will ever need. We don't need any more faith; we just need to use what we have been given.

If we are the children of the Living God, then we have all the power of the Godhead living in us. Just try to contemplate that just for a minute or two. The same power that created the whole universe is living in your body, the temple of God.

Another interesting thought to contemplate, is that we have the same Holy Spirit power as Elijah did when he called down fire from heaven.

> What? Know ye not that your body is the temple of the Holy Ghost which is in you, which ye have of God, and ye are not your own? For ye are bought with a price: therefore glorify God in your body, and in your spirit, which are God's.
>
> (1 Cor 6:19, KJV)

To be carnally minded is enmity with God.

> For as he thinks in his heart so is he.
>
> (Prov 23:7, KJV)

THE POWER OF THE SPOKEN WORD

When we repeat the words of Christ, we are standing in full agreement of the power of the spoken word. We come into line with the word in full agreement, believing that what is spoken *will* come to pass. Since the word of God is eternal, there is no limit to its power in time, space or matter.

If the technology had somehow existed in Jesus' time to have recorded the actual voice and words of Jesus, and we could play His voice back to the demons of sickness today, they would have to obey because they have to submit to the spoken word of Jesus. But we don't have to have a recording of His voice. We can just speak His words, through the power of the Holy Spirit, and get the same results.

The word is Spirit and life, and through the power of the Spirit, we can speak to any sickness in Jesus' name and it will leave, as long as there are not blockages to prevent this (see the invisible barriers to healing.) The spirits always obeyed Jesus, and through the mighty power in His name, they must obey you.

We have established that faith comes by hearing the word of Jesus, because Jesus is the word. If only we could grasp the power that is in the spoken words of Jesus. The spoken word contains the power to heal and save those who believe.

> The words that I speak unto you, they are Spirit,
> and they are life.
>
> (Jn 6:63, KJV)

THE POWER OF SPEECH

We are what we speak.

> Death and life are in the power of the tongue:
> and they that love it shall eat the fruit thereof.
>
> (Prov 18:21, KJV)

We speak what we believe in our heart.

> A good man out of the good treasure of his heart brings forth
> that which is good; and an evil man out of the evil treasure of

his heart brings forth that which is evil: of the abundance of the heart his mouth speaks.

(Lk 6:45, KJV)

There is power in our words and we reap what we sow.

One day, I might feel depressed, but that's only feelings. When we agree with those feelings by speaking it out, then it has gone from being a feeling to becoming a reality. Let's put it another way. You wake up in the morning and pray, and begin with praise. You thank the Lord for a good night's sleep, and in doing so you start the day by cultivating a thankful heart. I like to declare,

> This is the day that the Lord hath made, we will rejoice and be glad in it.

(Ps 118:24, KJV)

……..even if I don't really feel like it. By declaring this word, I am speaking positive things into my being.

But if you wake up one morning feeling tired, and maybe haven't slept that well, the devil might put a suggestion in your mind something like, "You're depressed aren't you?"

If you come into agreement with him, and start imagining all the things that you have to do that day, like going to work, or whatever responsibilities you face, you may feel overwhelmed even before you start. Before long, you will have come into agreement with the devil who only comes to rob, steal and destroy your joy in the Lord.

So when I wake up, I can choose who and what to come into agreement with; God's word of positive confession and gratitude, or the devil's distorted view of life.

There was a man in Bulgaria who had cancer. When he found out, he started declaring the word of God, believing the promises in the Bible for healing. He received faith by hearing the word spoken out loud, and just by hearing the word, began to renew his mind which gave him hope.

The healing scriptures that he heard, he repeated, then faith came and he was healed. He didn't believe at first, but the more he heard the word being spoken, the more the seed grew.

Speech was and still is the method used by God to create all things. Such is the power of the spoken word.

> Through faith we understand that the worlds were framed by the word of God, so that things which were seen were not made by things which do appear.
>
> (Heb 11:3, KJV)

> But without faith it is impossible to please Him: for he that comes to God must believe that He is, and he is a rewarder of them that diligently seek Him."
>
> (Heb 11:6, KJV)

Whilst Jesus was on earth, He taught us that through our speech, by proclaiming God's word through faith, we can move mountains. Was Jesus prone to exaggeration? Absolutely not. Jesus always meant what He said, and said what He meant.

> And Jesus said unto them, because of your unbelief: for verily I say unto you, if ye have faith as a grain of mustard seed ye shall (say) unto this mountain, remove from hence to yonder place; and it shall remove; and nothing shall be impossible unto you.
>
> (Matt 17:20, KJV)

Jesus knew He could move any mountain effortlessly. After all, He created them. Nothing was or is impossible for Him. But here, Jesus is teaching us that with the minimal amount of faith, we also can speak things into being, and that through our speech, when empowered through our little seed of faith, we can and will move mountains.

When we speak to a sickness in the body, the words we speak become empowered through Jesus' name. It's His name, and through His name alone that demons flee and sicknesses depart. Jesus wants us to put into practise what He taught us. Because the mother eagle on the cliff face knows she can fly quite effortlessly, she gently nudges her chick to spread forth its wings, encouraging it to do the same.

In the same way, Jesus is teaching us that through faith and by confessing the word, we can do the same things that He did. He actually said in one account that we will do more than He.

> Verily verily, I say unto you, he that believes on Me, the works that I do shall he do also; and greater than these shall he do; because I go to My Father.
>
> (Jn 14:12, KJV)

The Lord is clearly teaching here that we can speak things into being when mixed with faith in His name. All things are possible. It's our trust in the word to accomplish what we have spoken out in faith.

PART 2

HEALED BY JESUS

CONFIDENCE IN GOD

God is unchangeable, and His promises are sure, and His word is Spirit, truth and power. When we decide to step out in faith, and trust the Lord completely we discover that it is impossible for the Lord to somehow let us down, because His word cannot fail.

We can desire to put our faith into action, but desire alone will accomplish nothing. We have to know that God is with us and will accomplish, through our smallest amount of faith, what He wills.

I can categorically confess that whenever I have taken a step of faith, the Lord has never failed me and never will. This is the confidence I have in Him. I will explain what I mean by that. Let me give you an excellent example.

There is an account in the Gospel of Mark of a man who was sick of the palsy who was lowered through a roof by his friends to be healed by Jesus. They had no doubt whatsoever, that if they could just get their friend within healing distance of Jesus, he would be healed.

Jesus saw their faith, and He said unto the sick of the palsy, 'Son, thy sins be forgiven thee.'

(Mk 2:5, KJV)

These men had absolute confidence in Jesus and were willing to suffer the wrath of the house owner for dismantling his roof. Jesus didn't disappoint them. When we bring anyone to Jesus with even the smallest amount of faith, the result will always be the same. Faith in action results in healing.

When we look at all the healing miracles in the Gospel accounts, we notice that whenever anyone came to Jesus, even with the smallest amount of faith, there was always only one result. They were forgiven, made well, healed, and delivered.

A Roman centurion came on behalf of his servant. The centurion trusted Jesus implicitly. It was the centurion's faith, when put into action, that resulted in his servant being healed. He didn't want Jesus to come to his house because he felt unworthy, but said to Jesus

> I am not worthy that You should come under my roof: but speak the word only, and my servant shall be healed.
>
> (Matt 8:8, NKJV)

The point I want to make, is that whenever the sick were brought to Jesus in faith, they were healed. Whenever Jesus went to a sick or dying person's house, they were healed, or they were raised from the dead. We can have the same confidence today because Jesus changes not.

> Jesus Christ the same yesterday, and today, and forever.
>
> (Heb 13:8, NKJV)

I find the story of the Roman centurion all the more remarkable because, he was a gentile Roman soldier who had more faith and trust in Jesus than anyone in the whole of Israel. The Jewish religious leaders had religion. But this man had trust.

Jesus never turned anyone away. Again we see a woman putting her faith into action on behalf of her sick daughter in Matthew 15. She wasn't a Jewess, and Jesus had answered her

> I am not sent but unto the lost sheep of the house of Israel. Then came she and worshipped Him, saying, "Lord, help me."
>
> (Matt 15:24-25, NKJV)

As we read this account, this woman is willing to accept even the crumbs that fall from the Masters table.

> Then Jesus answered and said unto her, "O woman, great is your faith: be it done unto thee even as thou wilt, and her daughter was made whole from that very hour."
>
> (Matt 15:28, KJV)

A CRUMB IS ENOUGH

We see this woman's daughter set free from a demon after coming to the Lord. The woman came in faith, risking a rebuke because she was a gentile, but Jesus didn't see her race, He saw her faith.

My own personal testimony on the infallibility of God's promises was tested again when Ruth and I were cycling through France and were heading for Jersey, which is one of the channel Isles of the UK. We camped for two nights on a very pleasant French campsite next to the river. We were able to take a shower, and do some washing etc.

Early on the second morning, coming back from the showers, I noticed that there were a lot of German, French and Belgium number plates on vehicles. I was delighted to hear an English speaking voice coming from a middle aged woman standing outside her campervan with her husband.

I greeted them and asked them what part of England they came from. They seemed friendly and willing to talk. They asked why I was there so I told them that my wife and I were Christians who had been visiting many countries. I asked the woman if she believed in God. She said that she had a belief in God, but wasn't sure about some things.

I noticed that she was in great discomfort and pain whilst trying to support her back. I asked her how long she had had this back pain, and if she believed in the healing power of God. Again, she said that she wasn't sure. So I said to her, "Come over to our camp, and you will be healed," and we arranged a specific time.

I was all too aware that this woman had little or no faith, but can always rest in the knowledge that,

> No man can come to Me, except the Father which hath sent
> Me draw him: and I will raise him up at the last day.
>
> (Jn 6:44, KJV)

I always get so excited with anticipation of what is going to happen next. To our delight, she came over at the appointed time, and we all sat down together at a table. I explained that we were going to pray first, and then read a few passages of scripture to her, asking if that would be ok.

I always tend to read Mark chapter five, because in this one chapter alone we find a demoniac being delivered and set free, Jairus' daughter being brought back to life, and the woman with the issue of blood being healed.

After about three quarters of an hour of reading and expounding the scriptures to her, I asked the woman, "Do you believe that Jesus can heal you right now?" "Yes" she replied. "Yes I do."

Whenever I see even a spark of faith in anyone, it brings me sheer delight, because I know that they are going to get healed. It's a done deal. I asked the woman if she was ready for me to pray over her, and she smiled and said yes.

She received healing from the Lord instantly. Oh what joy it is to see someone delivered from pain and saved. There is no greater pleasure for me. I love to see the surprise on their faces when they realise the pain has gone.

We all rejoiced and gave thanks to the Lord for His healing and the woman returned to her camper. We will probably never clap eyes on this new saint of God again, but we will see her in glory. Praise be to the Lord.

THE FIRST HEALING

> Now faith is the substance of things hoped for, the evidence
> of things not seen. For by it the elders obtained a good report.
>
> (Heb 11:1-2, KJV)

How much faith do we need to be effective?

First of all, we see that faith is a substance. Let's compare it with water for example. Water is an amazing force. Floods can destroy anything that gets in its path. That is, in the natural world, as we understand it. Faith is a substance like water that starts with one drop, then becomes a slow trickle, and then a ragging torrent, where nothing can stand in its way.

We may think that we need a massive river of faith to move obstacles, but what does Jesus say?

> So Jesus said to them, "Because of your unbelief; for
> assuredly, I say to you, if you have faith as a mustard seed, you
> will say to this mountain, move from here to there, and it will
> move; and nothing will be impossible for you."
>
> (Matt 17:20, NKJV)

We only need the smallest minute drop of faith. God doesn't need a river. Taking a step of faith is not difficult when you have confidence, and know that the Lord always honours faith, no matter

81

how small, and that it is impossible for God to fail. So with that confidence, you can say to whatever mountain "Move," and it will move.

I will try and give you an example. The first time I experienced the healing power of God was about fifteen years ago. We were in a friend's house doing a bible study with a lady called Anne. This lady had just come to faith in Christ and was, what we would call, a young Christian, even though she was a mature woman. Ruth and I had only been saved about a year, so this walk with God and ministering by His Spirit was still relatively new to us.

We hadn't been in Anne's house long before she hobbled across the room and flopped into her chair. She was clearly in great pain as she grasped her knee.
"What's wrong?" I asked.
"I've been up most of the night in pain with my left knee" she said.
Then quite unexpectedly, out of the blue, I asked her "Do you believe Jesus can heal you right now?"

I was surprised myself at what I had said. Anne thought about it for a while and then said "I don't know." I knew she needed to hear the word of God, because by reading out loud the spoken words of Jesus, Anne would receive faith to be healed.

It was the first time I had ever done this, but I knew that the word could not fail in accomplishing what it wills. I had a quiet confidence that God wouldn't let me down, because God is true to His own word. Ruth began to read the words of Jesus, and then Anne said "well, that's it then. Will you pray over me Mark?"

I laid my hand on her knee, and said a simple prayer in Jesus' name. Not realising what had happened, Anne had been healed. We returned to our bible study, and when we had finished, Anne got up to go to the kitchen to make a coffee. She stood in the doorway to the kitchen with a big beaming smile on her face, waving her leg about with glee, and then we realised what had happened.

She looked quite surprised and was obviously healed.
"Mark you have healed me" she said. "No, I haven't" I said, "Jesus healed you, not me." That was the first time I experienced God's faithfulness for healing.

So from that moment on, I believed that God could heal any disease, and I became very excited about this new discovery.

A YOUNG MAN HEALED FROM ACUTE PNEUMONIA

I was sitting in my front room one morning, playing my guitar and worshipping the Lord, when I saw a vision in the Spirit. I saw myself praying over the young man who lived next door. His name was Damon.

I had tried to share my faith with Damon before but without much of a response. So when I saw the vision, although I knew it would come to pass, I couldn't understand why God would want to heal an unbeliever. But I thought to myself, I had better go and check it out.

I went to his house and knocked on the door. Damon answered, and I was shocked at his appearance! He looked like a dead man walking with a very pale complexion, and he croaked when he spoke.

"Hi Damon" I said. Obviously concerned about his condition, I asked him what the problem was. He said that he had been diagnosed with acute pneumonia, with fluid on the lungs. He explained that he was due to go into Blackpool hospital for specialist treatment, and an ambulance had been arranged to take him.

On hearing this I said to him "Damon, you know I am a Christian." "Yes" he replied. "Well, I can't explain this, but I believe Jesus wants to heal you right now. How do you feel about that?" I paused, preparing myself for rejection.

"Fine" he said. "If Jesus wants to heal me, then I won't need to have an operation will I?" Then he asked, "What do I have to do now?" So I replied, "If you come into my house, I will pray for you."

We both went back into my house and I told Damon to have a seat in the corner of the room while I went into the kitchen to get the anointing oil. As I began to pray over Damon, the Lord began to speak through my mouth which was one of the strangest experiences I have ever had. It was as if my lips would move with my voice but the Lord was speaking.

The Lord said to Damon, "Will you believe when you are healed?" "Yes, of course" he replied. "I will become a Christian, and you can baptise me Mark." My heart sank because the Lord had revealed to me that although Damon would be completely healed, he wouldn't believe and follow Christ, which I, for the life of me, could not understand. Then I realised the overwhelming compassion of Jesus.

The Lord knew Damon would not follow Him even though he was going to heal him completely. There is no condition to His love, just conditions to receiving salvation. What do I mean by this? The first condition to salvation is to believe, the second is to be willing to forsake everything and to follow Jesus, to do a u-turn on sin.

Without faith it is impossible to please God. If you don't trust that the Lord can save you then He never will. Even though I knew Damon had received healing when I prayed over him, I couldn't get my head around why Jesus would heal someone who refused the free gift of salvation. Damon thanked me for praying for him as he went back home.

As I pondered what had just taken place, I was very confused, because I had previously believed that if anyone had received a supernatural healing from the Lord, then they would automatically forsake everything to follow Him.

But I realised that this wasn't the case, as the Lord brought back to my mind the account of the ten lepers who Jesus healed, but only one had returned to give thanks, kneeling down to the Lord in worship, thanking and praising God for his healing.

> And one of them, when he saw that he was healed, turned back, and with a loud voice glorified God, and fell down on his face at his feet, giving him thanks: and he was a Samaritan.
> And Jesus answering said, Were there not ten cleansed? But where are the nine? They are not found that returned to give glory to God, save this stranger.
> And he said unto him, Arise, go thy way: thy faith has made thee whole.
>
> (Lk 17:15-19, KJV)

A few days later I got a phone call from Damon from the hospital. He was so excited he could hardly contain himself.

"I'm coming home" he said. "They were preparing me for an operation to extract the fluid from my lung, and not long after they got the results of my x-ray. The x-ray was completely clear, and they couldn't find anything. They are sending me home" he said.

I was obviously over the moon and in awe of God at what He had done. When Damon got home, he promptly went out playing pool in all the local pubs telling everybody he met that Jesus had healed him.

I learned a great deal from Damon's healing. God is far more willing to give than some are to receive. I learned to follow the Lords instructions even when I didn't understand what was going on. God wants our obedience, our trust and our willingness to, as Paul put it, be a fool for Christ.

When I knocked on Damon's door I was expecting rejection. I thought he was going to say something like, go away you fruitcake, or something on those lines. But to my utter shock and surprise, he believed, he received and was healed.

I also learned to take authority in Jesus' name over the sickness, by speaking directly to it and commanding it to leave. When praying with someone I always like to end with the scripture, by His stripes you are healed. I know the pain and suffering that the Lord endured in order to set us free. His blood was spilled to heal our wounds.

> He is despised and rejected by men, a Man of sorrows and
> acquainted with grief. And we hid, as it were, our faces from
> Him; He was despised, and we did not esteem Him.
>   Surely He has borne our griefs and carried our sorrows;
> Yet we esteemed Him stricken, smitten by God, and afflicted.
> But He was wounded for our transgressions, He was bruised
> for our iniquities;
>   The chastisement for our peace was upon Him,
> and by His stripes we are healed.
>
> (Is 53:3-5, NKJV)

I realised what amazing love and compassion Jesus has even for those who would reject Him, as is summed up in probably the most famous quote from the bible.

> For God so loved the world, He gave His only begotten Son,
> that whosoever believeth in Him should not perish,
> but have everlasting life.
> For God sent not His Son to condemn the world;
> but that the world through Him might be saved.
> He that believeth on Him is not condemned:
> but he that believeth not is condemned already because,
> he hath not believed in the name
> of the only begotten Son of God.
> And this is the condemnation, that light is come into the world, and men love darkness rather than light,
> because their deeds were evil.
> For everyone that does evil hates the light, neither comes to the light, lest his deeds should be reproved. But he that doeth truth comes to the light, that his deeds may be made manifest, that they are wrought in God."
>
> (Jn 3:16-21, KJV)

Praise God that forgiveness is available through Christ.

> But if we walk in the light, as He is in the light,
> we have fellowship one with another, and the blood of Jesus Christ His Son cleanses us from all sin.
> If we say that we have no sin, we deceive ourselves,
> and the truth is not in us.
> If we confess our sins, He us faithful and just to forgive us our sins, and to cleanse us from all unrighteousness.
>
> (I Jn 1:7, KJV)

Jesus healed Damon

THE MAN WITH DAMAGED SPINE

To God be the glory, for without Him we can do nothing. This next account was really a step into the bizarre. I was working for a very well known insurance company at the time. I had worked for them for quite a few years, and rejoiced in the fact that the Lord had opened up many opportunities for me to give the Gospel to my clients in their own homes. I half expected to get reprimanded by my supervisor because I often spent quite a lot of my client's valuable time sharing my testimony on how I got saved.

Part of my job was to go out in my car and find trades people, mainly builders, window cleaners etc, to sell income protection and life cover to. I used to approach people, who for instance, had to climb ladders as part of their work, as they were at risk of injuries if they fell off and would then struggle to pay their bills as a result.

One particular night, the Lord took my faith to a whole new level. I made an appointment with a joiner who had been working on a local building site. I travelled at the appointed time to his house and spent about two hours with him and his wife explaining the insurance policies and the details of claim entitlements.

They were a very friendly and hospitable couple, and having been reassured that they both understood the terms of their policy, I signed them up. I was surprised in the fact that I hadn't shared my faith with this couple, but as it was getting later in the evening, and I had spent so much time explaining the policies, I felt it was time to leave.

I picked up my briefcase and thanked them for their hospitality and made my way through the lobby out into the street. As we were about to part, I heard the Lord say to me, "Go back in."
Puzzled by this, and with slight hesitation, nonetheless I turned back to my host.

"Mike, would you mind if I stayed a bit longer?" I asked. I had already taken up most of this couple's evening, and I really didn't know what he was going to say. "No, not at all, come in. Would you like another coffee?" he asked. "Yes that would be brilliant" I said with a smile, not knowing what I was to do next. As he prepared our coffee, I sat on the settee and prayed quietly to myself. *Lord, I don't understand. What am I supposed to say now? HELP!!*

Mike came back into the room with our drinks, placed them on the table and asked something like…..."Why did you want to come back in Mark?" "Well" I said. "I can't really explain this, but I'm a Christian."

Immediately he interjected, to my relief, because I had no idea what I was going to say after that. He went on to ask me if I knew a man a particular man, who lived in the next town to where I lived. "Yes, I know of him" I said. "He says he is an evangelist. Do you know what that is?" "I know that this man prays over people with cancer and they get healed" Mike replied. With that, I said "God has given me a gift of healing."

I was quite astonished at what he had just said to me, because I could see that he believed in the miracle power of God to heal. He then went on to tell me that there was something wrong with his spine. He had been to different doctors and chiropractors and nothing had worked. He was constantly taking pain killers which brought little, if no relief.

He then asked me if I would pray over his back! "If you believe, then just receive from Jesus," I said. "I do!" he answered, "What do you want me to do?"

I asked him to have a seat on the settee; it was so bizarre to me. I could see his wife in the kitchen busy cooking, not aware of what was going on here. I did something that I had never done before with a non Christian, when praying over them for healing. I started speaking in tongues.

I was taken aback myself as I had never done this before with someone I didn't really know, but the Holy Spirit had completely taken over the events of that evening. I laid my hand on Mike's back and prayed, and after a few seconds he stood up on his feet. With a shocked expression on his face, he said "I'm healed. I'm healed, the pain has gone."

Then he said to me, without any prompting, "Mark, how do I get saved?" I invited him to kneel with me, and I led him through a prayer of repentance. We spent some time praying together, and he couldn't stop thanking me. "Thank Jesus, not me" I said.

I told him about a good church that he could go to as I finally left the house. I rang my wife Ruth straight away; I couldn't wait to tell her what had just happened. I was ecstatic.

The lesson I learned here was one of obedience through testing. I didn't understand why I had to go back into the house, or even if I would be welcomed back inside. But this I know, God knows everything. If we only obey without question, the results can be astounding. I thank God for this amazing testimony and it still thrills my heart to think on this event, even though it happened ten years ago.

What an amazing privilege to be used as an instrument for the Lord. God can only use is if we are willing to be obedient and a fool for Christ. Have I always been obedient? No. Am I a great man of God? No. I am just ready, willing and available for the Lord.
All glory, honour and power belong to Jesus.

DEAR JACKIE

The Lord had told me to go and visit our first church, as we had since moved on many years before to another fellowship. We thought it would be good to go back and visit our old brothers and sisters in Christ. We were welcomed back and enjoyed the meetings, and it was good to see that there were new faces there since we had left.

One bright sunny afternoon, we were walking through the town centre when we saw Jackie, one of the new faces from church. It was a lovely surprise to see her, she was on her lunch break so we stood and chatted for a while.

I couldn't help noticing that her wrist was in a bandage. She explained that she was finding her work very difficult as she had to carry trays as part of her work in a dental surgery. She wasn't looking forward to going back after her lunch as the pain in her wrist was getting worse.

"Jackie, you're a Christian aren't you?" I asked her. "Yes, you know I am" she replied. "Do you believe that Jesus can heal you right now?" I said. She thought about it for a while, and then said "Yes, I believe He can."

We were by some stone benches in the middle of town, so I asked her if she would take a seat, and if she would take the bandage off. Slowly she began to unravel it, and when her wrist was exposed, I held it gently and started to pray, and Jackie joined in agreement.

I told the wrist to be healed in Jesus' name, and heat went through my hand to the wrist. When I knew that the Holy Spirit had done His work, I asked Jackie, would you like to thank Jesus for your healing? And she bowed her head and gave thanks to the Lord for healing her wrist. I stood and asked "How does your wrist feel now?" I remember the surprised look on her face, and then the big smile that followed.

She held up her wrist and moved her hand round, "That is so much better" she said. She went back to work pain free and bandage free.

What a witness that must have been for her work colleagues. We saw Jackie at church at the next service and she was able to share with everyone how she had been totally healed and that her wrist was normal again. It was a great encouragement for everyone else.

It had taken faith for Jackie to remove her bandage. All you need is a seed of faith. That is sufficient for the Lord. A few years after that, Jackie went to be with the One who healed her wrist, the One who wipes away every tear and removes all pain and replaces it with joy and bliss.

CHILDLIKE FAITH

One summer's day in Nelson, Lancashire, I was in the centre of town handing out tracts. Ruth had to work that particular morning so I went alone. I didn't feel particularly spiritual, but I kept on praying for divine appointments, asking that the Lord would send a soul that was searching for truth.

I spoke to a few people and gave out some tracts, but nothing significant seemed to be happening. Then a young man came up to me, his name was John, he was very friendly. He was about forty years of age, wearing a flat cap and smelt of beer. After talking to John for a while he told me that he had a drink problem, and that he didn't have a job. He walked with a limp, using a walking stick to support himself.

I asked John if he believed in God. "Oh yes" he replied, "I was brought up a Methodist." I saw in John amazing childlikeness. He was a fully grown man, six foot plus, but had the heart of a child. I spent about an hour with John reading the scriptures to him on how to get saved.

I think I started in John 3, and went on to the book of Romans using the verses known as "The Romans Road." Then I did something I didn't normally do. I would have prayed for him there and then, but I wasn't compelled to do that on this occasion. Instead I gave John my address and said, "Come to my house and you will be healed."

I didn't want John to come to me, I wanted him to come to Jesus, and so I pointed this out to him. We used to hold a weekly bible study at our house, so we invited John to join us. When he didn't come the first week, I was disappointed. I thought to myself that many are called but few are chosen. We invite many, but we know only the chosen of God will respond.

To my surprise, one day I saw John walking up our street, I spotted him as he was looking for our house and my heart leapt for joy. The Lord had sent him! I contained my excitement enough to go outside and greet him and I invited him in. I read the bible to him, and when I felt that he was ready, or had faith, I asked him if he believed that he could be healed by Jesus. "Yes" he answered, so I took the anointing oil and prayed over him for his healing.

John received his healing from his dodgy hip, and when leaving the house he folded up his stick, put it away in his bag and literally ran down the street with great joy, praising the Lord. To me, there is no greater joy than to see the prisoners set free, glory to Jesus.

John started to come regularly to our house group on a Wednesday night. I used to love it when the Holy Spirit would completely take over the reading of the scriptures. Sometimes I would be told what to read, but didn't always know where to find that particular verse, but thank God I had quite a team of helpers, and a wonderful saint called Jenny, who was like a human concordance.

We once had to open all the doors in the middle of winter when the fires of God fell in our living room, wow it got hot and we all felt it! John had asked if he could bring his wife to the meeting the following week. "Of course" I said, "bring her by all means."

The next meeting, John brought his partner Jackie who we warmly welcomed. At the end of the meetings, I always asked if anyone needed prayer. Jackie stood up to receive, and as I started to pray over her for her healing, The Lord stopped me and said "No, I will not heal her because she has un-forgiveness in her heart for a man."

I was bemused by this revelation as I told Jackie what the Lord had just revealed to me. At that time, some weeks earlier I had been struggling when giving words of knowledge to people, and was so afraid with the fear of the Lord that I might get it wrong. I really didn't want to share what I knew with anybody else, especially considering that if I prophesy falsely I would be in deep trouble with God.

Over time the Lord comforted my troubled heart and gave me confidence to trust Him, so that when I gave a word of knowledge for someone I could have confidence that it was from God, and not just my imagination. If I had complete trust in Him then I could speak the oracles of God in faith.

So I said to Jackie, "The Lord won't heal you because you have unforgiveness for a man, do you know who it is?"
"It's my ex-husband" she replied. "He did this, and he did that….."
Relieved, I told Jackie to go home and pray, to repent of this unforgiveness, and pray for her ex-husband, then she would be healed.

Then the devil whispered in my ear, what if you're wrong and she's not healed?? Knowing that doubt is a weapon of the enemy, I dismissed the thought straight away, casting it down as Saint Paul said.

> For the weapons of our warfare are not carnal, but mighty through God to the pulling down of strong holds,
> Casting down imaginations, and every high thing that exalts itself against the knowledge of God, and bringing into captivity every thought to the obedience of Christ
>
> (2 Cor 10:5 NKJV)

I was totally blown away with what happened next. The following week, people started arriving for the bible study as normal, then another knock came at the door. It was Jackie, who had previously walked with two walking sticks, standing there with no sticks at all. I was totally gobsmacked and stunned, then a rush of joy filled my heart.

Jackie came inside the house. I couldn't wait to ask her what, how and when her healing had happened. Then I heard the Lord say to me in a crystal clear voice, "Why are you amazed?" I really had to stop myself and ponder at what the Lord had just said.

Jackie went onto explain that one night, after she had repented and prayed for her ex-husband, John suddenly turned to her and asked if she would like him to pray over her. She agreed, and her healing was the result! I was truly amazed, and the Lord knew it.

I think He was saying to me, you encountered me when you were fourteen, you have seen many people healed and you know that I can do anything, nothing is impossible for me. So why are you amazed?

From then on I stopped being amazed and started to totally rely on God, to expect the impossible was to be the norm from then on. Expectation is the key to faith.

Faith is not knowing that God *can* do it. Faith is knowing that He has *already* done it.

A MAN WITH CANCER

Whilst staying in Bulgaria in a little village for five months, Ruth and I got to know most of the poor gypsies in that area, and the appalling poverty they suffered.

One night we went to visit a bed ridden old lady who couldn't afford painkillers, and was so happy to receive some paracetamol. I have never seen anyone so grateful.

While we were there in her house, we got to know her son who was in his early forties. His wife already knew who we were and had great faith in the Lord. We learned that the man was suffering with cancer, he kept pointing to his chest and under his arm pit.

The cancer had spread, as far as we could understand in our limited Bulgarian, from under his arm pit to his lungs. I perceived that he thought he was going to die.

I told him "You are not going to die." The amazing thing was that Ruth was able to translate what I was saying by using a Bulgarian phrase book, and by using bible verses, read by the man's wife who was able to read and translate from her Bulgarian bible.

I asked him if he believed in God and he said that he didn't have a lot of faith. "Good" I said. "You don't need a lot of faith." Then I quoted what Jesus said, by pointing with my finger at the Bible verse in Mathew 17:20, that if you have the faith of a mustard seed, you can say to the mountain "Move," and it will move. I wasn't sure if he fully understood.

Although his wife looked worried, she was trying her best to hold onto her faith with everything she had. We asked the man if he would like us to lay hands on him and pray for him, and he willingly agreed, so we anointed him with oil and prayed over him in Jesus' name. Afterwards, I felt there was still something else we had to do.

When I went back to the house where we were staying, I felt I should print off all the healing scriptures in Bulgarian and give them to the man with cancer. I knew that faith comes by hearing the word, but he hadn't heard it yet because I couldn't speak his language properly.

So the next night, Ruth and I went back to the house. There were no street lights in the village, so we went with our torches in hand. We were again greeted like royalty. Because the man couldn't read, I gave the bible healing translations to his wife, and asked her to read them to her husband three times a day. I also told the sick man to repeat what he had heard.

Sometimes I do things that I don't understand, then try and make sense of it later. We said goodbye to our new friends, we ascertained that the man with cancer was going to the hospital for an x-ray and we would be back to see him on his return.

The following week, there was a loud banging on the iron gate at the front of the house. At first I thought it might be one of the gypsy children knocking, as they used to come for a banana or two. But this knocking was really loud.

"Mark, Ruth!!" shouted a voice. When I opened the iron door I was greeted by the sick man's son, and I will never forget his words. He said "Papa is crying, crying with joy!" With the very limited English he knew he said "Papa, hospital, x-ray, cancer finish!" He waved his arms, "cancer finished!" I just said over and over "Haleluyah, Haleluyah."

As I recall this event, I still fill up with emotion, because I saw the strain this horrible sickness had put on this family, but praise God for His everlasting mercy on us. Is God willing to heal all who come to Him? Absolutely.

What I have learned through this amazing healing first of all, was that this man wasn't a believer. I think he went along with it at first because he was desperate enough to try anything. He started off very fearful, and thought he was going to die, but God had other plans.

The man's faith increased the more his wife read the bible verses on healing to him. As well as hearing the words, he then proclaimed what he had just heard. If there is a lack of faith, there is a remedy!

> Faith comes by hearing, and hearing by the word of God.
> (Rom 10:17, NKJV)

Through the reading of the promises of God regarding healing, and through confessing them aloud in agreement that God is willing and able to heal and deliver, faith indeed came to this man, and complete healing was the result.

Praise the Lord for His goodness upon us, and His everlasting mercy!

ELIZABETH'S FAITH
PUT INTO ACTION

One night we got a telephone call from a very close friend who was extremely strong in her faith in Jesus. She had shared many stories with us over the years about the miraculous power of God that she had experienced, and how He had delivered her from danger many times when she lived in her home country, South Africa. She was now living with her husband Clive in a town fifteen miles away from us.

She rang us to say that she was in great pain and discomfort, and asked if we could come as soon as possible to pray over her for healing. We found out that she had had a fall and had been laid in bed for five days as a result. She hadn't been able to go to the bathroom, not that she couldn't get to it, but that her bowels had closed.

We went straight away, and saw our dear suffering sister lying in her bedroom. "Praise the Lord, thank God you have come." She was so grateful to see us, I knew she was in expectation of being healed. She knew not only that Jesus *could* heal her, but that she was *going to receive* healing from Him, and I knew it too. I knelt at the bedside and laid my hands on Elizabeth and said, "In Jesus' name of Nazareth, you are healed."

We said goodbye and left them, trusting that God would move, and as soon as we got back to our own home twenty minutes later, we got a phone call. We knew that she would be healed, but were surprised at the speed in which it had taken place.

"Brother Mark!" said our dear sister. "Oh brother, praise the Lord, the moment you left I went straight to the bathroom and was totally relieved, thank You Jesus!!"

Elizabeth was completely healed and delivered from all abdominal pain and discomfort, praise and glory to Jesus. She was so grateful to the Lord and it was so wonderful as always, to see a person set free from pain and restored to health.

This event was different to other healing accounts so far. Elizabeth was already a believer who knew the Lord and had faith in the power in His name to heal. It was a foregone conclusion that she was going to be healed. I didn't need to build her faith by reading the Word of God to her. The trust and belief was already there in her just waiting to be released.

Elizabeth's healing began the minute she picked up the telephone to call for prayer. Faith is an action, it does something. Picking up the phone was an act of faith that initiated her healing. Many times, Jesus told people to do something in order to activate their faith. He told a blind man to go and wash in the pool of Salome. As the blind man washed, he received his sight. His belief was put into action through obedience. He washed his face as Jesus had instructed and received his sight. Faith is active.

Jesus said to another man, to pick up his bed and walk. Here there are two instructions, both requiring faith which is carried out through obedience. I would go so far as to say that it is impossible not to be healed after putting faith into action.

I think a good idea would be to go through the bible and replace the word faith with action, or belief in action. Faith is never stagnant. To just believe is not enough, and this is what James meant by saying,

> Faith without works is dead.
>
> (Jas 2:20; NKJV)

Elizabeth

HEALED FROM DIABETES

When we spent five months in Bulgaria, we attended a large house church; it even had its own pulpit. It wasn't a particularly large house, but there were a large amount of people who met together in one room.

I was able to preach as the pastor from Chirpan had taken us there and could translate for us. My message was about how vital it is for us to forgive as Christ had forgiven us. At the end of my messages, there was always a time for people to be prayed for.

The lady who was hosting the meeting in her home came forward for prayer. She wanted healing from type one diabetes. I anointed her head with oil and prayed over her. She went a little wobbly, and then we thanked God for her healing.

There was no dramatic display, no falling down, just healing received by faith. She just felt the power of the touch of Jesus. She had responded to the message on unforgiveness, and had made a clear path for the Lord to bring healing.

I believe this woman had been held in the captivity of unforgiveness that can cause some forms of sickness. She, like many others was entombed; she had been locked there for many years. Although she believed in Jesus, and had prayed faithfully and gone to church, yet she was still held in a prison of sickness, and couldn't get out.

Unforgiveness is poison to the body. Does this mean that every sickness is caused by unforgiveness? Of course not. Why is it that people often weep when they forgive? It is because they have been carrying a huge heavy burden. The body will eventually buckle under its weight.

Unforgiveness and the unwillingness to forgive often manifests itself as sickness, and can lead to death through sickness. If we like it or not, unwillingness to forgive other people's offences is a sin. Jesus knew its destructive power over our lives and bodies, so He put its power to death on the cross.

However, although satan has been defeated, he can still keep us in a prison of bitterness, by our own choosing. Our own stubbornness and resistance to forgive will keep us bound. I want to show you, dear reader, that you can be free. Jesus said,

> If the Son therefore shall make you free, ye shall be free indeed.
>
> (Jn 8:36, KJV)

A Christian who isn't walking in victory over satan is not really free at all. We know that we cannot defeat satan in the flesh, we must rely on the power of the Holy Spirit, and so walk in the Spirit instead of the flesh. The Apostle Paul said

> I say then, walk in the Spirit and you shall not fulfil the lust of the flesh.
>
> (Gal 5:16, NKJV)

Let me share what happened to me and it might shed some light on why I know unforgiveness is so deadly. When I was fourteen, one night while I slept, I found myself in the presence of God. I was enveloped in   His love and I felt overwhelming joy. I didn't see the Lord, but I felt Him.

What was revealed to me on that night has had a massive impact on my life. There were people there who had perfect love for one another. There was no trace of resentment, bitterness or unforgiveness. There was a total absence of anything evil, and perfect love was in its place.

I had experienced a taste of paradise and I can't wait to go back because I know it's real. I feel so privileged to have been allowed to taste the overwhelming love of Jesus. In the Bible account of the night that Jesus was arrested in the garden of Gethsemane, we see Peter taking his sword and with it He chops off the ear of Malchus, the servant of the high priest.

The love of Jesus is shown here, even in this dark scene, when He touches the face of a man involved in his arrest, and heals him on the spot. His mercy is true and active even on His enemies. Jesus never paid evil for evil; He overcame evil with good, and demonstrated this as well as teaching it.

If we want to follow the Master's way, then we must do the same. Love your enemies, do good to those who hate you. Jesus wasn't just a preacher of the right way. He first preached on how to overcome satan and walk by faith, then He demonstrated it.

Jesus said "I am the way, the truth, and the life." It's quite simple really. If we walk His way then we will be saved by faith in Him.

The result is being born again, and we will be able to forgive our enemies because

The love of God is shed abroad in our hearts.

(Rom 5:5, KJV)

Healed in Bulgaria

THE MAN WITH PROSTATE CANCER

During a five month stay in Bulgaria, I had the opportunity to preach in the Sunday service in a church in Chirpan, around eight miles from where we were staying. The young pastor of the church spoke English well enough to be able to translate for me.

After the service, I asked that those who would like prayer should come to the front of the church, and I was amazed by the response. Almost the entire congregation came forward; they were so thirsty for God.

One of the men who came forward wanted prayer for healing from prostate cancer. I laid my hands on him and prayed, but nothing happened. He knew it and I knew it. The Holy Spirit had revealed to me that there was a blockage preventing his healing, so I suggested to the man that we both spent the week seeking God as to what the hindrance was, and then to meet again the following week. He smiled and agreed.

Very quickly the Lord revealed to me that the blockage for this man's healing was witchcraft. The next week came, and after the meeting the man with prostate cancer came forward for prayer again.

"Did you ask the Lord what the problem is?" I asked. "Yes" he replied. "Witchcraft." It is wonderful how the Holy Spirit works.

I asked him where it was from. He explained that his Grandmother had practised witchcraft, being involved in the occult. Although this man wasn't involved or responsible, the Grandmother had brought a curse upon the whole family. We see in the bible that sins practised by family members can have an effect on us.

> For I the Lord thy God am a jealous God, visiting the
> iniquity of the fathers upon the children unto the third
> and fourth generation of them that hate me.
>
> (Deut 5:9, KJV)

Once the hindrance had been revealed, it was possible for us to pray with results. The man renounced witchcraft, and instead of praying for healing, the generational curse was broken through the power in Jesus' name. The result of this was that the man was healed immediately.

In this instance I learned that you cannot heal a demon, you have to cast it out. The demon of sickness will not be broken until the cause of entry has been renounced, then and only then can the curse be broken. Demons must be commanded to leave, and curses have to be broken through renouncing it.

Because of God's grace, Christ became a curse for us when He hung on the cross. A curse on any family can be broken, and we can be delivered from the effects of any curse. The man with cancer was cured. The curse was brought in to the family by the Grandmother, and as a result I believe the whole family came under that curse.

People dabble with the occult, many not realising the dire consequences of their actions. If people would only read the Bible and take it for what it says then they would fear the Lord and stay well away from any form of the occult.

There are many that open a portal to satanic forces in pure ignorance. I did this myself after my Mother died with lung cancer, about ten years before I got saved. A friend asked me to attend a Spiritist meeting where they supposedly contact our dead relatives. Many people are under the impression that Spiritism is of God, but it is not.

Vulnerable people are given false comfort in believing that their dead relatives are speaking to them. In actual fact it is the demons who are controlled by satan that are working through a spiritualist to deceive these poor people by imitation. The demons imitate our dead relatives, seducing people into thinking that they are indeed talking to their dead loved ones.

If you have been involved in this subtle deception and want to break free from the curse it may have brought on you, then you need to repent and renounce it, speaking out audibly in prayer to the Lord, asking for forgiveness.

You must acknowledge and renounce your involvement in the occult. Your sins will be forgiven as long as you are sincere. If you need any help or advise with this I strongly recommend you go to your nearest Pentecostal church and ask the Pastor to pray over you. He will know what to do.

Mark and Mitco

THE SIKH MAN HEALED
OF PSORIASIS

God will never fail us. He will never reject our small amount of faith. He will not despise us, He will only add to our little seed of faith. Jesus brought the Kingdom power of God to earth. He demonstrated the Kingdom's awesome power time and time again; power over any disease.

This particular healing event taught me so much. I met a Sikh man who was selling mobile phones on the inside market in the town where I lived. I got chatting with him, his name is Bopal and he seemed very friendly and open to talk.

After telling him my name, not wanting to waste time, I got down to business. I asked him about his faith and what he believed in. He went on to briefly explain that he was a Sikh, and that he had many gods. Then he asked me who my god was.

"Jesus" I replied. "He's my God." Then I got a revelation from the Lord that led me to ask about his wife's sickness, which then led on to him proclaiming that both he and his wife were sick.

I asked what the problem was. Bopal told me about his wife's many sicknesses, and then his own. He had psoriasis all over his body. I asked him how he had got it, which I thought was a bit of a strange question.

"Oh" he said, "A witch doctor put a curse on me when I was a young man in India." Then he asked, "Can Jesus heal me?" "Yes" I said, with sheer delight. I went on to explain that Jesus became a curse for us so that we might be healed.

Then he really challenged my faith. He asked "Would it be possible for me to come to your house after I finish work, and if I come will Jesus heal me?" I said "Of course He will heal you, because He is God Almighty." So we arranged for him to come at about 6.30pm.

In my experience, there have been quite a few people that I have invited to come to the house but not everyone has the faith to put into action. But this man's faith blew me away. At 6.30 he knocked on the door and I invited him in.

"Hello, welcome" I said. "Do you want tea or coffee?" "No sir" he gestured, clasping his hands together. I was absolutely amazed with this man's faith. My wife Ruth was introduced before going upstairs to intercede in prayer.

I invited Bopal to take a seat while I sat on a chair about five feet away from him. At this point I would have anointed him with oil and laid hands on him, but I'm quite sure that the Holy Spirit had completely taken over the following proceedings, that literally left me speechless.

Knowing that faith comes by hearing the word, I asked Bopal, "Would you mind if I read the bible to you?" "No, not at all" he said.

I opened the bible, I think I was looking for John 3 but opened at John 1. I began to read from the start of the chapter.

> In the beginning was the word, and the word was with God, and the word was God. All things were made by Him.
>
> (Jn 1:1, KJV)

Then to my astonishment, I glanced over at Bopal, and he was obviously in the presence of God. He was holding his arms up in the air, shielding himself as though from a bright light saying "Oh my God, my God" over and over.

Then he said, "Mark, I feel so peaceful." I was totally taken aback by what I was witnessing before my very eyes. "Praise God, Haleluyah!" I said. He then held up his arms in the air and looked in astonishment, he said to me, "I have been healed!"

Bopal had come for his healing and The Lord didn't disappoint him because he believed and received. He said to me, "Mark, how do I get saved?" So I knelt on the floor and beckoned him to join me. I led him in the prayer of repentance which he did straight away. It was an amazing time of celebration

> Likewise I say unto you, there is joy in the presence of the angels of God over one sinner that repents.
>
> (Lk 15:10, NKJV)

What I have learned from this, is that normally I had to lay hands on people and pray for them in order for them to receive healing from the Lord. But the Lord was showing me the power of speaking the written word. Bopal had amazing faith when he knocked on the door, but the healing power came through speaking out the written word.

Jesus didn't just lay hands on the sick; He *spoke* to the sickness, commanding it to leave. It left through the power of the spoken word. Jesus had been given authority and power to raise the dead, to cast out devils and to heal all manner of diseases.

Jesus also had power over the elements. He stilled the storm and walked on the water. There was nothing that He could not do, and there is nothing that He cannot do today. Jesus gave His authority to us.

> Behold, I give you the authority to trample on serpents and scorpions, and over all the power of the enemy, and nothing shall by any means hurt you.
>
> (Lk 10:19, KJV)

There is no special qualification needed to read out loud the word of God, administer anointing oil, or to lay your hands on the sick. The only qualification needed is a seed of faith, and God will do the rest.

RAISED FROM THE DEAD

Jesus said that all things are possible for those who believe. All things means that nothing is impossible. I want to share what happened at our church in Manchester one Saturday morning. It's a messianic fellowship called Sulam Yaacov, meaning Jacob's Ladder.

We had been praising the Lord in our meeting during the praise and worship time, enjoying and experiencing the presence of God. We had been in worship for about forty five minutes when suddenly one of the worship leaders stopped the music and was pointing to something I couldn't see behind me.

I looked over my shoulder and an elderly lady whose name is Margaret, was slumped in her chair as one dead. As soon as people saw, they started to gather around her, stretching out their hands in prayer. Someone rang for an ambulance, her lips were blue, her breathing had stopped, and there was no pulse. This woman was completely dead.

I lifted her from her chair and carefully laid her on the floor, and instead of doing CPR, I laid hands on her and prayed over her. The whole church was praying for a miracle. Her pulse was checked and rechecked by a lady called Susan who had been a nurse, and was knelt down at the dead woman's feet.

I asked Susan if there was any pulse and she said no, shaking her head. There was nothing, she wasn't here anymore. Still expecting God to move, I looked up at John the pastor and asked for the anointing oil, as it's written in James to pray using oil.

> Is any among you afflicted? Let him pray. Is any merry?
> Let him sing psalms. Is any sick among you? Let him call for
> the elders of the church and let them pray over him, anointing
> him with oil in the name of the Lord.
> And the prayer of faith shall save the sick, and the Lord
> shall raise him up: And if he have committed sins, they shall be
> forgiven him.
>
> (Jas 5:13-15, KJV)

He quickly returned with the oil and he anointed the dead woman on her head and we prayed over the body. We knew Jesus had power over death, and that death could not hold this saint. At that moment it was announced over the P.A. system that there was a red car blocking the entrance for the ambulance. By this time Margaret had been dead for at least ten to fifteen minutes.

Thinking it could be my car, I quickly went outside to the front where I had parked, but there was no sign of the ambulance. I thought to myself that it must have gone to the back of the church, so I went to investigate.

I saw the paramedic rush through the side entrance where my dear friend Les was standing in tears. "Are you alright?" I asked Les. "Yes" he said, smiling. I couldn't understand why he was smiling with tears in his eyes. "Looks like she's gone home to be with the Lord Les" I said, trying to comfort him. "Oh no" he said. "She's sat up smiling."

Not knowing what had just happened to her, Margaret was more concerned that she had disturbed the meeting than anything else! It seemed like almost everyone in the church wanted to know if she had been to heaven, because they knew she had died.

God is always doing those things that are hard to believe. But I know the Lord brought Margaret back to life that day. Let all the glory go to the resurrection and the life, Jesus.

Margaret

THE HUNCHBACK CAT

The story I am going to share next is probably the one that people will find the hardest to believe. I can assure you that I found it hard to believe myself at first! But since I know that nothing is impossible for God, I know it's true.

One day I was prospecting for business in my local area when I thought to myself, I need to travel further afield. I had pretty much exhausted work contacts in my home town, so I headed for the motorway in my car to the next big town. But as I approached the off ramp, I felt a prompting to keep on going.

I drove on to the next big town after that, and then the same prompting happened again. Forty five minutes later I came to the Manchester slip way heading for the city centre, and felt a sudden impulse to turn right, which leads to the back road at the side of a very large park.

As I drove up that road I saw a bicycle shop on my left. I was building a bike at home at the time and needed some parts for the project, so I pulled in at the shop and parked the car. It was a pretty old bike shop that looked like it had been there for years. I walked in and started browsing around to see if I could find what I was looking for.

There were a couple of customers in the shop initially, but they soon began to leave and I was left alone with the shopkeeper. I approached the counter and asked if he had what I was looking for. He gave me the part, I paid for it, then I was about to ask him if he believed in God.

Before I could utter a word, he asked me "Do you believe in miracles?" I had never met this old gentleman before, I thought it quite strange. Unbeknown to him, as a born again Christian who believed whole heartedly in miracles, I was curious to find out more. So my reply to his question was "As a matter of fact I do believe in miracles. Why do you ask?"

He introduced himself as John, and asked if I had a few minutes to spare as he had a story he wanted to share with me. Of course I said yes, and so he began to tell me about an incident that had happened in his shop about thirty years ago. John had been going through some very hard times financially and was on the verge of bankruptcy.

He owed a huge amount of money to the income taxman and had run the stock right down in his bike shop. At the same time his wife was in hospital battling with cancer. He went to tell me that he was only taking about fourteen pounds a day, it just wasn't sufficient to keep the business afloat.

One day, while he was working at the back of the counter, he just collapsed under the weight of his overwhelming circumstances and found himself on his knees. When in total despair, he said he just cried out to God.

"God, if You are there, I need Your help right now!" He got back on his feet, and faced the rest of the day. John was a Catholic.

I was getting excited at this point. He went on with his story, I was gripped. He told me that not long after he had prayed, a man came into his shop. "That racing bike in the window" the man said. "Can you get it down, I want to buy it?" It was a really expensive bike.

"Don't you want to have a look at it first?" John asked the man. "No, that's fine, I'll take it please." "How do you want to pay for it?" John asked: amazed at what was happening.

The man brought out a huge wad of money from his pocket and put it on the counter. In today's value it was worth about £1000. The customer happily took his bike and left the shop. John was staggered at what had just happened. The day continued and not long after many more people came in and bought more bikes. Customers came in throughout the day, and spent a staggering about of money until he closed.

I just kept saying "Wow, wow, that's amazing!" John had been able to clear a large part of his debt straight away through one day's takings. I couldn't help but rejoice at what the Lord had done in answering this man's prayers so speedily. I thought that was the end of the man's story, and I was about to leave to do some work when he carried on telling me about another miracle that had happened in his shop.

He told me that a stray cat came into his shop one day. It had a hunch on its back and a large abscess on its backside. The poor cat meowed in pain when it walked, and he wanted to do something to help. Still listening with great interest, John told me that he took the cat to a vet who said that there was no hope for the cat, and that the kindest thing to do would be to put it to sleep.

He told the vet that he would take it home for a week, and if there was no improvement he would bring it back. I was totally unprepared for what he was about to say next. He said that he had been reading a book by an evangelist, and it was written in this book that if we have faith in Jesus, we can pray through Jesus' name over any person who is sick and believe that they will receive healing, and that the person would recover.

So he took hold of the poor cat and began to pray for its healing. The cat suddenly leapt out of the man's arms and landed on its feet. John then told me how the hunch straightened itself out before his very eyes and the abscess on it's behind burst open and began to leak out onto the floor.

It took me some time to absorb this amazing event. Knowing that nothing is impossible for the Lord, I believed John's story, and thanked him for sharing that with me. I left that shop that afternoon on a spiritual high.

The Lord had sent me to John's shop for encouragement, and for me to give him the Gospel. Belief is so rare to find these days, as the days grow darker. That is why it is so important to share the good news today, because we do not know if we have tomorrow.

I have since learned that John has gone to be with the Lord, and I'm looking forward to seeing him again in paradise with his cat.

DEAR RUTH

My wife and I had been helping at an evening children's club at a nearby church. One night as we were leaving, saying goodnight to the little ones and their parents, a woman approached me with a question.

"Excuse me" she said, "Are you a Christian?"

"Yes I am" I said. "Why do you ask?"

"Do you believe in the devil, and demons and things?" she continued.

"Yes of course. If we believe in Jesus then there has to be a devil doesn't there?"

"Can I tell you what happened to me?" she asked. I listened intently.

"I was in my bedroom one night when a great darkness fell on the room, and I saw the devil and demons. I was terrified" she said. I could see that she was so desperate for someone to believe her story and to take her seriously.

"I believe you" I said. "Carry on." She was so glad and overjoyed as she continued, asking repeatedly "You do believe me, don't you?"

She then went on to explain that she was so afraid that she cried out to the Lord Jesus and at that moment a light filled the room, and the devil was gone.

I had experienced the supernatural power of God in dreams and visions, so I didn't have a problem believing her. On reflection, I felt a bit like Jesus with the woman at the well. She was so thirsty for living water.

I asked her if she wanted to come to our house group and learn the bible. With great enthusiasm she said that she would love to and we exchanged names and she took for our address.

This lady was called Ruth. Ruth came every week and heard the word of God, and we spent time with her regularly as she lived quite near to us. It was wonderful to watch her grow in faith.

Thinking back, I realise now that Ruth had been born-again on the night that she had called out to Jesus in her bedroom. The bible says that he who calls on the name of the Lord will be saved. She was like a sponge who couldn't get enough, and was always asking questions and eager to learn more.

One night, after our bible study meeting had finished, people started to go home, until just Ruth was left behind. My wife went into the kitchen to make drinks and I was left alone with Ruth in the lounge.

I felt the Lord saying to me to anoint Ruth with oil, to stand back and then to blow on her. I was very reluctant to do this because I had seen Benny Hinn do this on the television. Knowing him to be a fake, I was very wary and wanted to test all spirits, as taught by John in 1 John 4:1

I was wrestling, you might say, with the Lord's instructions. Eventually, I shared with Ruth what the Lord had just said to me.

"That's fine" she said. So we both stood; I anointed her head with oil, then I stood back and blew on her. I didn't know what to expect to be honest. Ruth started shaking and then bent over and started to cough, then she straightened up and took a big breath of relief.

We were both surprised at what had taken place. I realise now that Ruth had many demons of addictions. She had been battling with heroin and alcohol, and had been suffering for many years. After the blowing incident, and the anointing of oil, Ruth was completely delivered from her addictions and was filled with the Holy Spirit.

Ruth had been delivered dramatically, with no withdrawal symptoms, no cold turkey. She was totally free and knew it. She was so happy and couldn't get enough of the presence of God. My wife and I prayed over her new house that Ruth had been given by the Lord, all was going so well and there was much excitement as we saw God move in Ruth's life.

If she ever felt tempted she would ring us and we would pray together. I had a gut feeling that Ruth was going to fall again, but I knew not to despair because the battle belongs to the Lord. I suppose I wanted her to overcome so badly, but we couldn't fight her battles for her.

One day after several weeks, she visited an old friend and the temptation took over. She took heroin and was unconscious for three days. It was days later that we heard about this. Obviously we were so sad at what had happened, but I had a quiet reassurance that the Lord had won the victory over Ruth, and that He wouldn't leave her or forsake her.

Although she had fallen, she went on to spend time in a rehab and is now going on stronger than ever with the Lord. We recently found out that she is running a support group called Families in Recovery and all that attend have got saved and are following Jesus.

It is written that a righteous man falls seven times. I hope Ruth's battle will give encouragement to those who are battling from any form of addiction, from gambling to pornography, or even food. Jesus died to set us free from the power of the devil. The devil has to let go of his victims when the Lord shows up.

There is no greater power in the universe. He came to save us, not to condemn us, and to deliver us from anything that has control over us.

One drop of His blood has more power than all the demons and the devil put together.

A WOMAN DELIVERED FROM DEMONIC DREAMS

When Ruth and I lived in the North of England, we ministered to many people who were suffering from a wide range of addictions, mainly heroin and alcohol. Our home was open for anyone who needed help.

One day a woman in her forties with a big drink problem called to the house and asked if we could come and pray over her home as she was having demonic dreams, and had been for some time.

We asked if she'd had any involvement at all in the occult. She was surprised at first and then shared with us her interest in the supernatural. We shared with her what the bible says about fortune telling, and speaking to 'the dead,' and asked her if she would be willing to renounce all forms of witch craft and to practice them no more. Of course she was willing.

Next was to pray and bless her home, so Ruth and I visited and suggested that all objects related to the occult be removed and destroyed before praying over the rooms in the house.

What we found there was unbelievable and quite disturbing to say the least. The house was full of Buddha's and demonic plates of every kind imaginable, crystal balls, tarot cards and occult books. I asked the lady, "Do you want the devil out of your house?" "Oh yes" she replied.

So I started to fill a black bin liner with these items, going from room to room. This lady had it all, and it all went in the bin. She was reluctant to part with some items because they had been gifts from family and friends. We went through the entire house and came down stairs, and we all sat in the living room.

"Is that everything?" I said. "Yes" she replied. Then I felt the Lord was showing me that there was still something left upstairs. "Are you sure there isn't anything left upstairs?" I asked.

Then she admitted there was one thing that hadn't been detected; yet another demonic plate with symbols on it. She reluctantly surrendered it to the bin. We came back down the stairs and my wife Ruth noticed a pendant hanging around this ladies neck and asked what it was.

"Oh!" replied the lady, "That's my crystal. I ask it questions, like, shall I go out with this boyfriend or another?" In absolute astonishment we told her that it had to go.

Eventually she saw the danger in talking to a demon spirit through a crystal pendent. As we prayed with her, she began to see just what she had been involved in, then we prayed in every room and blessed the house.

Guess what? The dreams stopped, and she slept in peace.
If you have been involved with any form of the occult, then first you need to repent to the Lord Jesus, acknowledging your sin, and then you need to renounce all forms of the occult and walk in newness of life.

BILL AND THE ELUSIVE WOMAN

Ruth and I had been led to live in a flat in a converted church for three years. The Lord had provided it through a lovely old gentleman called Fred who was moving out of his church flat into sheltered accommodation. It had been his son Peter, who we knew from our local church that had invited us to go and have look at it. We were praying for somewhere new to live at that time.

God provided amazingly for us as no deposit was required, and Fred was leaving most for the furniture behind for us to use, including kitchen crockery and pans etc. We were both astonished and so grateful. It was a great place to live, and we were able to give the good news to many people while we lived there.

Not far from our flat, we were able to witness to a good hearted man called Bill in his home. Jean, his wife, seemed to be really friendly but would never want to socialise with us. She would make us a drink in the kitchen, bring it to us and then disappear again. Ruth had tried to befriend her without much success.

Bill had been an alcoholic for many years, and we would tell him of the power of Jesus to set prisoners free. At first I felt that we weren't getting anywhere with him. His attention span was short, and Bill would often wander from the conversation.

He would tell us stories of how he had jumped from helicopters whilst serving in the army, and how he had damaged his leg doing this. He showed us photographs of those days, and I felt such compassion to see this man healed and set free. So we kept trying to steer the conversation back to Jesus.

"Bill, do you want to be set free?" I asked him one day. "Will you pray with us and ask Jesus to forgive your sins?"

But like most people he couldn't face reality and had turned to the demon drink. Having been a borderline alcoholic myself, I was passionate to see Bill delivered. We had known Bill for almost a year and, to be honest, I didn't think that we had got through to him, but I was wrong.

The word had got through to him. The following week we visited him again and talked for a while, then to my surprise he suddenly fell to his knees and wept his heart out, asking Jesus to forgive him. Afterwards he was just hugging me.

As I recall this now, I feel myself welling up, because not long after this had taken place, Bill went to be with the Lord, but I know I will see him again. I was stunned and saddened when I found out, but I remembered and rejoiced over the night that he repented before God, and was reassured that Bill was safe on that golden shore.

When I found out that Bill had died, I called around to the house a few times hoping to see and comfort Jean, his widow, but could never get a reply. I was determined to keep trying. Then, one Sunday afternoon after we had just returned from church, I had left Ruth at the flat as she prepared dinner, and I walked around the corner to see if Jean was at home.

As I knocked on the door, nothing could prepare me for what was about to happen next. Jean opened the door and looked directly at my face, unlike at previous occasions. I was dumbfounded at what I saw. Her face contorted in multiple deformities, it's the only way I can describe it.

Then I understood through the Holy Spirit that Jean was demonized, and that the demons in Jean were reacting to Jesus in me. It's not every day that Christians encounter these sorts of things. Some Christians unfortunately never experience the supernatural world at all, and this saddens me as more people could be delivered if they only believed.

My first reaction on Jean's doorstep that day was shock and fear. Then the word of God came to me straight away.

> Greater is He that is in you, than he that is in the world.
>
> (1 Jn 4:4, KJV)

Almighty God in us, through the Holy Spirit, is greater than the devil and all demonic power who were defeated at the cross.

I was pretty inexperienced at dealing with demons in those days, so I quickly asked if I could call back later and left. I went home and called for reinforcements in the shape of Pastor Frank who lived about seven miles away. He had spent time in Africa and had a great deal more experience than I in the deliverance ministry.

I rang him and told him what had just happened with Jean and asked if he could come and help. He came over straight away. Ruth, Frank and I went to Jean's house that same afternoon, not knowing what to expect.

I knocked on the door and Jean answered, she stepped back in fear when seeing us stand there. We introduced Pastor Frank, and he spoke to her in a gentle voice asking if it was alright for us all to come in, and that we were only there to help.

To our relief she invited us in. We went into the lounge where Jean sat down as Pastor Frank asked her if it was alright for us to pray for her, she agreed. Before we started to pray, Frank asked her a question.

"Jean, can you say Jesus is Lord?" She opened her mouth and tried to say the simple words but nothing came out, she couldn't say it! We hadn't seen anything like this before.

At that point, Frank began to speak to the demons in her, and we were praying and speaking in tongues, commanding the demons to leave. I had seen the movie "The Exorcist," this was nothing like that. It was, nevertheless, very intense and dramatic to us. I remember feeling quite excited at seeing the result of demons coming out of Jean, but I was a little bit green in those days.

Ruth and I started singing a song called 'There's power in the blood,' knowing that the demons are terrified of the blood of Jesus. Frank carried on commanding them to leave, and Jean's small framed body lurched forward from her seat as each demon left, then she would slump back again, looking quite exasperated.

Frank asked the original question several times throughout that afternoon, repeating again "Jean, can you say Jesus is Lord?" Frank explained to us later on that no one can say Jesus is Lord while they are demonized, because Jesus is not their Lord.

About two hours had passed by, when we finally saw Jean released from the last demon. We knew it was finished simply because Jean was able to say at last that Jesus is Lord. We were all exhausted and very relieved when it was finally all over.

We asked Jean if she knew any hymns so that we could all praise God together. We then spent some time singing and praying, and praising God as we prayed for Jean to be filled with the Holy Spirit. After praying and time with Jean, we left her at peace with God, rejoicing at what He had done.

A few days later, I went to a shop nearby, parked my car just outside on a quiet street, when Jean unexpectedly appeared walking towards the shop. She didn't look like herself anymore. The much aged, tired looking Jean now appeared twenty years younger. I shouted over to her, she waved with a big smile on her face, and I thought to myself, she looks like an angel. Isn't it amazing what God can do?

THE DEMONISED
LITTLE BOY

Ruth and I had been visiting a single mother who lived on our street. She hadn't lived in her house very long and was in a very bad situation. Someone had kicked the panel in the front door of her house, and the boiler was broken on her central heating along with a multiple of other problems.

One night we called in to see how she was, we were seeing how we could help and offer some support as well share the Gospel with her. She invited us in and we spent some time playing with her little, five year boy had been diagnosed with autism. We were able to talk with her about the Lord Jesus and share with her how He was able to help anyone spiritually, physically and emotionally.

This lady was completely overwhelmed by her problems and started crying in despair. We wanted to help in any way we could. I said to her, "If you ask Jesus to help you, He will." I asked her if she could pray and just ask God for help, and she couldn't.

She suddenly got a breakthrough and was able to pray, calling on the name of the Lord with tears. We stayed and comforted her, encouraging her that God had heard and would answer.

A few days later we noticed she had a brand new door. She invited us in and was so happy to show us the new boiler that had just been fitted as she told as about the things that had happened in such a short time since praying for help. We were so happy as we praised God together.

While we were talking, I lifted her young son up into my arms to play as we had done before. His mum had explained to us that he had never spoken a clear word since he was born. He made sounds and noises but no comprehensible words. This boy was definitely not autistic.

I swung him around a few times as he laughed with enjoyment, and then I placed my hand on his head and said "In Jesus' name." I hadn't finished my sentence when he pushed himself out of my arms and shouted in a very aggressive and clear voice "Get off me, get off me!!"

His mother was both astonished and petrified. She was clearly amazed as she heard her little boy speak for the first time, but shocked at the words that had come out from him. With as much sensitivity as possible we tried to find out more about her son. "He throws himself down the stairs" she said.

Immediately I remembered the account in the bible of the man who came to Jesus saying that his son was tormented by a demon that often threw him into the fire. Jesus was able to cast the demon out of the man's son and restore him to a sound mind, but we were unable to minister to this little boy, because the mother was so frightened by what she had just seen that she asked us to leave.

We tried to explain that there wasn't anything to be afraid of, but to no avail, but we continued to pray for his deliverance. As Jesus said,

This kind can come forth by nothing, but by prayer
and fasting.

(Mk 9:29, KJV)

Sometimes we feel so helpless, but the Lord can do far above anything we ask and pray for. So in Him we trust, because after all the battle belongs unto the Lord.

This lady moved house again shortly after, and we were unable to keep in contact, but we are still believing for the mother and child's salvation.

JACK AND MAGDALENA

In 2013, Ruth and I cycled to Bulgaria through eight countries which took us two and a half months. After spending the winter in Bulgaria, we boxed up the bikes, and flew on to Israel. We felt this was the mission God had planned for us.

Before we left England to start our journey, a Polish man in our fellowship had told us that we must visit his home church in Poznan. We had no idea where this city was at first, but saw that Lord might be leading us through this man. We planned our route accordingly, making contact with the church, sending emails to let them know that we were coming.

Although it was a massive diversion, we couldn't take the chance that God wasn't guiding us through this Polish brother, as we know that God, at times, uses people to direct our paths. Sometimes we can miss what God is telling us to do, as we don't always have ears to hear, although I would not take notice of everyone who said they had a 'word' from the Lord for us. We don't always get it right, but thank God for discernment through His Spirit.

After enjoying the scenic cycle paths of Holland and Germany, we found that the roads in Poland were so dangerous in comparison. After a short time in this country, we thought it best to hop on a train and head straight for Poznan where the church would be waiting for us.

When we arrived, after unloading the bikes and panniers, we saw that there was nobody there to meet us. I thought to myself, *this is strange. I know God has sent us here, so where are they?* We hung around the station for a little while, looking for a waving hand or a smiling face of welcome, but we saw nothing.

We decided to find a café with wi-fi internet to see if we had received an email from the church. Still no reply, and nobody was answering the phone. Realising that we were alone in this massive city was a bit daunting, to say the least!

When it seems that our plans have failed, the Lord is always there to guide the way. Oh what a wonderful Shepherd we have.

We prayed and asked the Lord to intervene, and that's exactly what He did. Not long after we had finished praying, a man on a mountain bike rode up to where we were sitting and said, in fairly good English, "Hi, nice bikes, where you from?" "England" I replied.

I started to explain that we were Christians and had hoped to meet people from a local church, but we couldn't seem to get in contact.

He then stated that he was a Christian, so I asked him if he was born again. "I am Catholic," he said. "My name is Jack." I explained to him that I used to be a Catholic, and then I got saved.

"Saved, what is saved?" he asked, so we invited him to sit and have a coffee with us while we answered his question and shared the gospel with him. He then said, "Where you stay?" "We don't know" I replied.

Jack asked us if we would wait at the cafe for fifteen minutes or so, after which he would return. "Yes, no problem" I replied. He telephoned a female friend of his, before riding off on his bike across the busy main street, promising to return soon. We just sat, waiting and wondering what was going to happen next.

Twenty minutes later, Jack returned with a big smile on his face and said that his friend, Magdalena, would like to invite us stay with her. We graciously accepted and happily followed Jack on our bikes, winding through the many streets, and crossing busy sets of traffic lights.

After being led through many short cuts of the city, we arrived at a large apartment block where we met our hostess, Magdalena.
The bikes and equipment were stored in the cellar, and in good English, Magdalena warmly invited us into her apartment, saying that we were very welcome to sleep on her pull-out sofa-bed for a couple of days.

During our stay there, we expounded the Bible and shared testimonies of what God had done for us; Jack and Magdalena were so thirsty to drink of the wells of life.

While gathered for our evening meal, I noticed that Jack wasn't eating anything, and I asked him why. To which he replied with a grimace, "No," gesturing with his hand, "I have problem with stomach."

Empathising with him, I asked "Jack, do you believe that Jesus can heal you?" He paused for a while then thoughtfully said, "Yes, I do." I asked him if he would like us to pray over him, and he eagerly agreed. Ruth got out the anointing oil and we prayed over Jack in Jesus' name.

To the glory of God, the following morning Jack ate a full breakfast! What joy it brings to see a person freed from their affliction. Jesus had completely healed Jack, and we all rejoiced in what the Lord had done.

I had also noticed that Magdalena had been holding her back in pain, and I asked her the same question. "Do you believe Jesus can heal you right now?" "Yes" she said, and again, after prayer, she too was healed. The pain had left her back.

We left the following day after praying with our new-found brother and sister, telling them they needed to arrange to be baptised by full immersion according to the scriptures, with their local Pentecostal church.

So, it was God's plan for us to visit Poznan after all; He had led us to these wonderful people and His will was done. What amazes me is that out of the vast population of this massive city, we were sent for just theses two people, Jack and Magdalena.

What joy it brings to see the Saviour release the captives, Is 61:1.

To God be the glory.

Jack

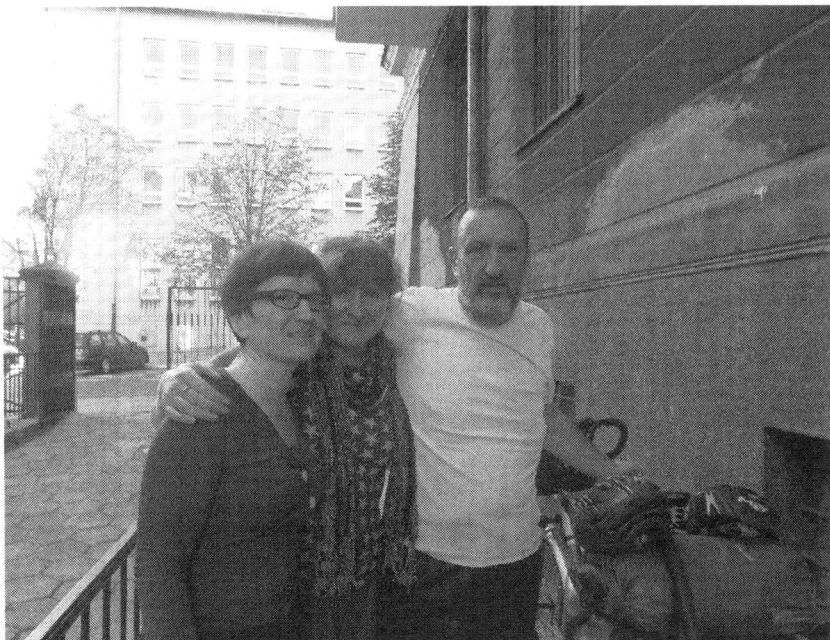

Magdalena, Ruth and Mark

PART 3

THE MAIN INVISIBLE

BARRIERS TO HEALING

THE MAIN INVISIBLE BARRIERS TO HEALING

As I will explain in more depth, you do not need a lot of faith to be healed; you only need a mustard seed. But there are invisible barriers that prevent Jesus, and His life giving Holy Spirit from healing and delivering people. Many think that if only they had more faith they would be healed. All believers have more than enough faith, but there is something that is blocking that healing power from getting through.

I have found through personal experience that we need to do some soul searching detective work through the illumination of the Holy Spirit, allowing Him to search our hearts. He can reveal to us what the blockages are. I have listed the main barriers to healing, and they are as follows.

A. Un-forgiveness resentment and hatred
B. Unbelief
C. Ignorance
D. Occult Involvement
    1. Fortune-telling
    2. Ouiji board
    3. Horoscopes
    4. Superstition
    5. Freemasonry and Orange order Rock music
    6. Drugs
    7. Spiritism
    8. Witchcraft

    10. Druidry

    11. Divination

    12. Necromancy

F. Family generational curse

G. Idolatry, idol worship

H. Unconfessed sin

I intend to expand on all the major barriers to healing with a prayer of repentance following each one. I suggest that you don't just speed read, or skip over what you consider irrelevant, because you may miss something very important and vital to you. I would even suggest following this book with a note pad and pen and read the passages that I have suggested, to get a deeper understanding.

I can't stress enough the importance of prayer, because without it nothing is going to happen. I would also include fasting but consult your doctor first. Jesus came to provide a way to be healed and delivered physical, mental and emotional healing.

> The Spirit of the Lord is upon me, because He hath anointed me to preach the Gospel to the poor; He hath sent me to heal the broken hearted, to preach deliverance to the captives, and recovering of sight to the blind, to set at liberty them that are bruised.
>
> (Lk 4:18, KJV)

> For this purpose the Son of God was manifested, that He might destroy the works of the devil.
>
> (1 Jn 3:8, KJV)

Jesus has provided healing for all that would come to Him and believe. Not only does He want to heal, but is in the process right now, at this very second, healing somebody, somewhere in the world.

Jesus said,

>My Father works hitherto, and I work.

(Jn 5:17, KJV)

God is always working day and night,

>He neither slumbers nor sleeps.

(Ps 121:4, KJV)

UNFORGIVENESS

Do we know what is buried deep down in our hearts? The answer may come as a surprise to some, as the answer is no. We don't really know what is in our own hearts.

> The heart is deceitful above all things and desperately wicked, who can know it?
>
> (Jer 17:9 KJV)

We can see in the next verse that only God knows what is in the heart.

> I the Lord search the heart. I try the reigns, even to give every man according to his ways.
>
> (Jer 17:10 KJV)

If our own hearts are deceitful then it is able to hide the truth and deceive us into believing a lie. You may hold resentment and unforgiveness towards a person, or several people, and not even be aware of it.

Unforgiveness is like poison that gets into the blood stream and makes the body sick. A root of unforgiveness causes bitterness to spring up, often at the most unlikely moments, and manifests itself through anger or resentment, and ultimately leads to various forms of sicknesses. It not only affects our bodies, but causes damage in our relationships, even with those that we love.

I have seen multiple healings take place after there has been open confession of unforgiveness. It is possible to build up unforgiveness for a number of people over the years, even from things that occurred in childhood. I believe unforgiveness often results in sickness in many forms, and ultimately leads to death, because all unforgiveness is sin.

159

> For the wages of sin is death; but the gift of God is eternal life through Jesus Christ our Lord.
>
> (Rom 6:23, KJV)

There is a great release that takes place when a person makes a decision to forgive someone, and I have seen people delivered from many types of sicknesses when they prayed for their offender's salvation.

In the account of Job in the bible, we can see how he had held resentment and bitterness for his so-called friends during his great trials. But when he softened his heart towards them, the Lord who sees our hearts released Job from his captivity, breaking the stronghold of satan, who had held him prisoner for a long time.

> And the Lord turned the captivity of Job when he prayed for his friends.
>
> (Job 42:10 KJV)

STELLA'S STORY

This next account taught me so much about unforgiveness and the power that it has over us. It was a beautiful sunny day, and my wife and I had arranged to meet an evangelist and his son in law to join together and share the Gospel in Blackpool town centre. The evangelist had a microphone and an amplifier, and was sharing Gods word to those passing by while Ruth and I handed out tracts.

We had many good conversations with people, but there was one woman in particular who I will never forget. There were many people coming and going in the busy shopping centre, and we had handed out many tracts. I handed a tract to a lady who was walking past, and in an aggressive manner, she refused to take one, and carried on walking away.

The Holy Spirit clearly said to me "Go and follow her." I literally ran after her, thinking to myself, *what am I doing?* I caught up to her

160

and walked alongside, and said, "One minute of your life, that's all I want." She was obviously still perturbed from my first feeble attempt. She turned to me, as if to say, "Not you again?"

"What do you want?" she said in a strong Northern Irish accent.
"I want to give you the good news!" I exclaimed.
She replied in a most aggressive tone, "What good news?"
"The good news of Jesus Christ" I said.
"I'm a catholic, I already believe in Jesus" she replied.

I was going to show this angry lady some bible scriptures when suddenly the Holy Spirit gave me insight into this woman's heart. I stepped back. "What is all this hatred you have in your heart?" I asked. To my surprise, she broke down and started to weep.

"What's your name?" I asked, wanting to try and comfort her.
"Stella" she said.
"What is it Stella?" I asked.

She began to tell me as she wept, that the IRA had killed both her parents in the Enniskillen bombings. My heart immediately went out to her.

"I can't imagine the pain you must have suffered from your loss, and now I completely understand where your anger and hatred has come from. But holding this hatred in your heart for the people who did this will only destroy you and make you sick. Jesus knows your sufferings, but He also wants to heal your broken heart and give you life."

"How?" she asked. I opened the bible at John 3 and explained that we all need to be born again to enter the Kingdom of God, and for the Kingdom of God to enter us. She had never heard this before, even though it is a clear commandment of Jesus. I said to Stella that she needed to forgive those people.

"I can't" she replied, "I just can't."

"No, you can't on your own" I said. "But if you let Jesus into your heart and repent of your sins, He will help you to forgive, and He will forgive you your trespasses through the power of the Holy Spirit."

I could see hope in her eyes as she said, "I will do it, I'll do it right now." "Go home" I said. "Get on your knees and pray, repent to the Lord. But I should warn you that satan will try and stop you." I will never forget her reply.

"Nothing or nobody will stop me from praying," she said. With that, she dried her eyes and gave me hug before walking away. I often wonder how many others are suffering like Stella. I believe that our meeting was preordained, and that she was able to forgive and receiving forgiveness and healing in her heart.

Jesus went around preaching the good news that everyone who comes to Him will be forgiven and healed, healing takes place in the soul first. If you read the accounts in all four Gospels, everyone who came to the Lord was healed. His blood still holds the same power to heal; it will never lose its power. One drop of Jesus' blood is more powerful than the whole kingdom of satan.

Anyone who calls upon the name of the Lord will be saved. This is a cast iron guarantee from the Lord of all truth, that He is faithful to cleanse us from all sin. Holding anything against anyone reveals the true condition of a wicked heart. It is an unwillingness to show mercy, setting itself as judge, jury and executioner.

There are some people who expect to be forgiven for a life time of sins but are still unwilling to forgive one person's offence that may have been festering in the heart for many years. This double standard is totally unacceptable to God, to ask Him for mercy but being unwilling to be merciful.

If a man say, I love God, and hates his brother, he is a liar·
For he that loveth not his brother whom he has seen, how can
he love God whom he hath not seen.

And this commandment have we from Him, that he who loveth God love his brother also.

(1 Jn 4:20-21 KJV)

If you are struggling because you've been deeply hurt, just consider Jesus' sufferings before and on the cross, when He was able to say, even in excruciating agony,

Father, forgive them; for they know not what they do.

(Lk 23:34, KJV)

Jesus is willing to forgive us through His amazing grace towards us. Peter asked the Lord a question regarding forgiveness.

Lord, how often shall my brother sin against me and I forgive him? Till seven times?

(Matt 18:21, KJV)

I suppose Peter thought himself to be very generous in his willingness to forgive seven times. But what is Jesus' reply?

I say not unto you until seven times, but until seventy times seven.

(Matt 18:22, KJV)

This is 490 times! Does this mean that after the 491st offence you can stop forgiving him Peter? Absolutely not. Forgiveness is to be continuous and without limit. Jesus wasn't putting a boundary on forgiveness. Instead, He was giving an example to show the true condition of Peter's hard heartedness, in thinking it generous to forgive seven times.

If you want to break free from the bonds of bitterness and unforgiveness, ask the Lord to help you, He will make you able.

Humble yourselves therefore under the mighty hand of God that He may exalt you in due time. Casting all your care upon Him; for He careth for you.

(1 Pet 5:6-7, KJV)

Holding resentment and unwillingness to forgive is satan's way, not God's way. Satan wants to keep us in bitterness. Have you noticed that when you try to forgive someone, satan will bring to mind their offences over and over again, and he will try to revive old feelings to make it harder for you to forgive?

> Be sober, be vigilant; because your adversary the devil, as a roaring lion, walketh about, seeking whom he may devour.
>
> (1 Pet 5:8, KJV)

> And they overcome him by the blood of the lamb and by the word of their testimony.
>
> (Rev 12:11, KJV)

We know that we can overcome and win in this struggle to forgive. I have found that speaking out my willingness to forgive is effective. In speaking, we are confessing to a great multitude in the heavens of our willingness to show mercy, which in turn defuses the power of satan to hold us in captivity.

Love and compassion are greater than hate. It was love that held Jesus to the tree; it was love that conquered satan for you and for me.

PRACTISING THE PREACHING

> And when ye stand praying, forgive, if you have ought against any: that your Father which is in heaven may forgive your trespasses. But if ye do not forgive, neither will your Father which is in heaven forgive your trespasses.
>
> (Mk 11:25-26, KJV)

Whilst praying one day, I was staggered to say the least, at what the Lord was about to reveal to me. He was about to show me what had been hidden and laid buried in my heart over my entire life time.

Only God knows what is in our hearts.

> I, the Lord search the heart, I try the reigns, even to give every man according to his ways, and according to the fruit of his doings.
>
> (Jer 17:10, KJV)

The Lord told me to get a piece of A4 paper and a pen, and that He was going to reveal the names of several people who had caused me all kinds of deep physical, emotional pain throughout my life. So I took a pen, and the Lord took me back in my mind to my childhood years, and I wrote down several names of people, until I had around twelve listed.

Their offences came back to me, and I was able to recall memories, some very painful, of events that had taken place many years ago. The amazing thing was that I had absolutely no memory of the things being revealed until the Lord revived what I had chosen to forget.

I felt the Lord then impressing on me to forgive each person one by one, and then pray for their salvation, asking the Lord to forgive them.

I was surprised at some of the memories that I had forgotten about. I remembered a friend from my youth, whose father owned a farm. One night we were taken to a local pub after a full day of hay making, even though I wasn't yet old enough to drink.

I had bought myself a new pure wool, grey coat which I treasured. When I went to get my coat from off the hanger inside the pub, it wasn't there. It had been stolen. Ten years later, my farming friend confessed to me that it was he who had taken my coat, and then apologised. He must have had a guilty conscience.

Many years later as a Christian, I was being reminded of this event. I had held a deep resentment and had unforgiveness for my old friend, even though he had admitted his offence and said sorry.

I had forgotten about it, but God hadn't. At last I was able to forgive him and I prayed that one day he might get saved.

I followed this same pattern for everyone on my list. It is also vital to forgive yourself, as God does not want us to live with guilt and self-condemnation.

> If the Son, therefore shall make you free, ye shall be free indeed.
>
> (Jn 8:36, KJV)

> There is therefore now no condemnation to them which are in Christ Jesus
>
> (Rom 8:1, KJV)

I would strongly recommend this to every Christian on the planet. Pray and ask the Lord to show you if there is anyone in your heart who you are holding unforgiveness towards, and start writing as the Lord leads you.

King David knew that he couldn't see into his own heart. That's why he prayed,

> Search me, O God, and know my heart: try me, and know my thoughts: And see if there be any wicked way in me, and lead me in the way everlasting.
>
> (Ps 139:23, KJV)

UNFORGIVENESS PRAYER OF REPENTANCE

Father God, I acknowledge that I have sinned against You, and You alone. I ask You now to search my heart and reveal to me any person that I have held resentment, bitterness and unforgiveness for.

I repent of my desire for revenge, and ask that You would cleanse me of my all my sin. I renounce it now, and I lay it down at the foot of Your cross.

I chose to forgive *(it is important to name the person)*_____ for what he/she did to me, and I ask You Lord Jesus to forgive them and bless them.

I ask that You would replace the bitterness in my heart with Your love for _____.

Thank You Lord for Your willingness to forgive me as I forgive others, and I ask for Your supernatural healing on my body, soul and spirit.

I thank You Lord that You have heard my prayer

In Jesus' name, amen

UNBELIEF

Everything that is not of faith is sin. It is sinful not to believe God and take Him at His written word.

Have you ever told somebody the truth and they didn't believe you? How do you think God feels when you don't believe Him and His word? If the Truth told you the truth, and you didn't believe that truth, are you not then making the truth a lie?

Not believing God is the same as calling the Truth a lie. By saying God doesn't tell all truth is the same as calling Him a liar, and making His word false. It is impossible for God to tell an untruth, or to make a promise that was false. Therefore we can have confidence in His word.

It is also impossible for satan to tell the whole truth, because he is the father of lies. We all have a choice to trust God or satan.

> But without faith it is impossible to please God.
>
> (Heb 11:6, KJV)

FACING DOUBT

Jesus said, "I am the way, the truth and the life." Jesus didn't only *speak* all truth; He *is* the personification of all truth. He told His disciples that He would rise from the dead after three days, so why did they doubt Mary Magdalena when she proclaimed the truth to them that Jesus had risen from the dead, and she had seen Him alive?

169

The spirit of unbelief had crept into their hearts, and they had listened to its voice instead of remembering what their Lord had said and promised. The key to faith is to refuse to listen to the voice of doubt.

When Peter walked on the water, he was able to do the impossible because he set his eyes on Jesus, and he trusted the Word. The second that he took his eyes off Jesus, doubt entered in and he began to sink. The only way to dispel doubt is to have absolute trust in Jesus, knowing that He will never fail us.

> If Christ be not raised, your faith is in vain; ye are yet in your sins.
>
> (1 Cor 15:17, KJV)

Since we know that Christ is risen, we can have confidence that our faith is not in vain, and we can trust the whole of God's word and purposes for our lives.

> He that spared not His own Son, but delivered Him up for us all, how shall He not with Him also freely give us all things?
>
> (Rom 8:32, KJV)

In a nutshell, all unbelief is sin; get rid of it and choose this day to believe. Jesus will never fail you. God's promises cannot be broken; His word cannot fail to come to pass when mixed with our mustard seed of faith.

FAITH IS TRUST IN ACTION

The word for *faith* in Greek, *Pisti* implies action.

Even so faith, if it hath not works is dead, being alone.
Yea a man may say, Thou hast faith, and I have works:
Shew me thy faith without thy works, and I will shew thee my
faith by my works.
For as the body without the spirit is dead, so faith without
works is dead also.

(Jas 2:17, 18, 26, KJV)

Personally, I think the wording in James doesn't reflect in the English language what James is trying to teach us. It might be better understood if we were to replace the word *works* with *action*. For example, a Jehovah's Witness has been deluded to think that he/she can obtain salvation through good works, and therefore have twisted the true meaning in this passage. A better way to interpret this verse should read, faith without putting it into action, is dead.

God will not despise your little faith. He will increase it with each step as you choose to put it into action. We can say with confidence, "I might not understand but I choose to trust the Master, because I know He cannot and will not fail me. Even though I might have the smallest amount of faith, I know that with it I can say to the mountain move, and it will move."

Jesus didn't just teach a doctrine. He demonstrated the power of faith through His actions, not just to prove that He was sent from God, but to teach His disciples how to put their faith into action and do the same as He.

Verily, I say unto you, he that believes on Me, the works that
I do shall he do also, and greater works than these shall he do;
because I go unto My Father.

(Jn 14:12, KJV)

Jesus trusted His Father implicitly, that He could not let Him down.

Jesus said,
> All things are possible to him that believes.
>
> (Mk 9:23, NKJV)

Jesus didn't say that some things are possible, He said all things. That means that nothing is impossible. The word of God cannot be broken. It cannot fail. Doubting Jesus is tantamount to rendering Him untrustworthy, and we know that He is not. We overcome by the words of our testimony and the power of the blood. I recommend quoting this scripture,

> The Lord has not given me a spirit of fear, but of power and of love, and a sound mind.
>
> (2 Tim 1:7, NKJV)

Because unbelief is sin, we need to acknowledge it for what it is, and not try to excuse it.

> The Lord's hand is not short that He cannot save, nor is His ear deaf that He cannot hear. But your sins have separated you from your God.
>
> (Is 59:1, KJV)

If you have been plagued with unbelief, not trusting God, then you need to repent. There is hope for you. Satan would like you to believe otherwise, but he is the father of lies.

REPENTANCE PRAYER

Father God, I come to You in Jesus' name and I confess my sin of unbelief. I do not try to excuse it.

I am responsible for it, I am sorry for it. I ask You to forgive me and to deliver me from it, and I ask that You impart to me Your faith.

I want to declare: I believe in God the Father, the Son, and the Holy Spirit. I believe in the bible, the true word of God,

In Jesus' name amen.

IGNORANCE

Some people say, what you don't know won't hurt you. But is that true? I recently read a true story of a snake catcher in Zimbabwe who had been bitten by a banded cobra snake. He had continued to chase the snake for ten minutes before he suddenly dropped dead.

The tragedy in this story is that the snake catcher had a vial of antivenom in his pocket. He knew it was there, but he never used it because he didn't realise the snake venom would pump through his body so fast that it would kill him before he got a chance to administer the antivenom.

If the man had stayed still and taken the antivenom, he would be alive today. The same is true for many people today. They have a sickness called sin running through their veins. That sin causes no end of problems and miseries including sickness and death.

> For all have sinned and come short of the glory of God.
> (Rom 3:23, NKJV)

> For the wages of sin is death; but the gift of God is eternal life through Jesus Christ our Lord.
> (Rom 6:23, NKJV)

Thousands of people are sick and dying without the knowledge that can save and heal them. Unfortunately, many are ignorant of the cure; that Christ has paid for in full, because they have never read His words in the bible.

175

My people are destroyed for the lack of knowledge.

(Hos 4:6, NKJV)

Jesus said,

Come unto Me, all you that labour and are heavy laden, and I will give you rest. Take my yoke upon you, and learn of Me; for I am meek and lowly at heart: and you shall find rest unto your souls.

(Matt 11:28-29, NKJV)

The remedy for all sickness is in the bible, but through ignorance many are unaware of what the Lord has made freely available. There is an easy solution to this, and that is to study for yourself.

To deliberately ignore, or disregard as unimportant the word of God, is sin. Since all unconfessed sin separates us from God, we need to confess it as sin.

IGNORANCE PRAYER OF REPENTANCE

Father God, I acknowledge that I have sinned against You, and you alone.

I come to You now in repentance and acknowledge that I in many ways am ignorant of Your word, and of Your will, through my own fault.

I confess it as sin, I repent of it and ask You to forgive me, and ask that You help me to seek the truth more diligently from now on.

In Jesus' name, amen.

UNCONFESSED SIN

When we get saved through faith in Christ, we are forgiven completely from all our past sins that we have ever committed. This is only the beginning of our new life in Christ. Although we are saved, sealed in the Holy Spirit, we are constantly being changed and sanctified daily into the image of Jesus from the inside out.

We cannot expect to become like Christ overnight. It takes time for the Holy Spirit to increase as we decrease, surrendering our will to the Lord's perfect will.

Jesus didn't just die on the cross to save us from hell; He died to empower us to overcome all sin in our lives.

Although sin cannot separate us anymore from the love of God, unconfessed sin will be a hindrance in our walk, and will block any healing from being received. Sin that is kept in the dark will give the devil a stronghold in our lives, our conscience, emotions, relationships, and our bodies.

God has many blessings and benefits to pour out on His children.

Bless the Lord, O my soul, and forget not all His benefits:
Who forgives all your iniquities; Who heals all your diseases,
Who redeems your life from destruction; Who crowns you with
loving kindness and tender mercies.

(Ps 103:2-4, NKJV)

The only thing that will block the blessings and healing power of God in our lives is sin. When we get rid of the sin through confession and repentance, bringing it into the light, then the blessings come in.

> If we say that we have fellowship with Him, and walk in darkness, we lie, and do not the truth: But if we walk in the light, as He is in the light, we have fellowship one with another, and the blood of Christ His Son cleanses us from all sin.
> If we say we have no sin, we deceive ourselves, and the truth is not in us. If we confess our sins, He is faithful and just to forgive our sins, and to cleanse us from all unrighteousness.
> If we say that we have not sinned, we make Him a liar, and His word is not in us.
>
> (1 Jn 1:6-10, NKJV)

> For God sent not His Son into the world to condemn the world; but that the world through Him might be saved.
> He that believes on Him is not condemned: but he that believes not is condemned already, because he has not believed in the name of the only begotten Son.
> This is the condemnation, that light is come into the world, and men loved darkness rather that light, because their deeds were evil.
> For everyone that does evil hates the light, neither comes to the light, lest his deeds should be reproved. But he that does truth comes to the light, that his deeds may be manifest, that they are wrought in God.
>
> (Jn 3:17-21, NKJV)

The more we seek God and read His word, the closer we will be to Him. If we neglect to read and study His word, we will very easily fall back into our old sinful ways. You can get the people out of

Egypt but getting Egypt out of the people is something that only God can do.

If we are not sure if there is a sin blockage blocking the blessings, then we can ask God.

> Behold, the Lord's hand is not shortened, that it cannot save; Nor His ear heavy that it cannot hear. But your iniquities have separated you from your God, and your sins have hidden His face from you, so that He will not hear.
>
> (Is 59:1-2, NKJV)

God can save in the blink of an eye. Salvation is never earned by our good works. Our good deeds would never be enough to obtain salvation for ourselves. This would be like saying, Jesus died for 75% of our sins, but our good deeds will pay for the other 25%.

No, only the sinless Saviour would be allowed to atone for our sins because He is 100% perfect.

The high priest of old had to declare the sacrifice spotless and clean to be able to cover the sins of the people. Any lamb that was flawed by having any blemishes whatsoever would be rejected.

Jesus didn't come to cover our sins, as the Old Testament sacrifices did. Instead He came to take them away once and for all. John the Baptist declared this of Jesus,

> Behold! The Lamb of God, who takes away the sin of the world!
>
> (Jn 1:29, NKJV)

The devil has deceived the world into believing we are all good. If you were to ask one hundred convicted prisoners who are currently in jail if they were innocent or guilty, I believe most of them would declare their complete innocence, and blame someone else for their incarceration.

Even though they were found guilty through over whelming evidence by the jury and court, they somehow cannot admit their guilt. Some might make excuses by blaming their upbringing, or their parents, so they carry on being self deceived, and cannot face up to their true condition.

But when the light of the Gospel shines upon a willing heart, the Holy Spirit illuminates their darkened mind and reveals their sin. The only solution is to be willing to ask the Holy Spirit to search your heart and see if there be any wicked way in it, then be ready and willing to repent of any sin that the Lord reveals to you.

PRAYER OF REPENTANCE
(By King David)

> Search me O God, and know my heart: try me, and know my thoughts: and see if there be any wicked way in me, and lead me in the way of everlasting.
>
> (Ps 139:23-24, KJV)

INFANT BAPTISM

Another barrier for salvation and healing is infant baptism, or Christening. I believe many have been deceived into this false doctrine that is not scriptural, and are under the illusion that they and their children are eternally secure when this couldn't be further from the truth.

You see, you cannot see the truth, (forgive the pun) without the Holy Spirit, who promises to guide us into all truth. But the unfortunate reality is that many Church denominations are still practising this unbiblical heresy, and therefore many are spiritually dead.

The Holy Spirit will not reside in a church that has deliberately gone into heresy. They have had their lamp stands removed, the Holy Spirit has departed.

> Remember therefore from where you have fallen, and repent
> to do the first works; or else I will come unto you quickly, and
> will remove your candlestick out of its place, except you repent.
> (Rev 2:5, NKJV)

Nowhere in the bible does it mention infant baptism or christening. In these last days, and I do firmly believe that we are in the last days, the bible says there will be a falling away from truth, and this is what we can see in the age that we live in.

> But there were false prophets also among the people, even as
> there shall be false teachers among you, who privately shall

bring in damnable heresies, even denying the Lord that bought them, and bring upon themselves swift destruction.

(2 Pet 2:1, NKJV)

THE ESSENTIAL NEED FOR ADULT BAPTISM

There is a lack of understanding about baptism and why we need to be baptised as adults, and not as children. Jesus came to show us the perfect example to follow. He was thirty years of age when He was baptised by full immersion.

The fact that John used a river to baptise, and that it had to be deep enough to submerge a man or woman, proves without a shadow of a doubt that people were fully immersed by total dunking. You don't need a lot of water to sprinkle on the head. You do, however, need enough water for people to be fully submerged.

And John also was baptising in Aenon near to Salim, because there was much water there: and they came, and were baptised.

(Jn 3:23, KJV)

SO WHY THE NEED FOR TOTAL IMMERSION?

We find the answer in Romans 6.

Know ye not, that so many of us as were baptised into Jesus Christ were baptised into His death?
Therefore we are buried with Him by baptism into death: that like as Christ was raised up from the dead by the glory of the Father, even so we should also walk in newness of life.
For if we have been planted together in the likeness of His death, we shall be also in the likeness of His resurrection:
Knowing this, that our old man is crucified with Him,

182

that the body of sin might be destroyed, that henceforth we should not serve sin. For he that is dead is free from sin.

Now if we be dead with Christ, we believe that we should also live with Him: knowing that Christ being raised from the dead dies no more; death hath no more dominion over Him.

For in that He died, He died unto sin once: but in that He liveth, He liveth unto God.

(Rom 6:3-10, KJV)

One other point to remember is that John the Baptist called baptism a 'baptism of repentance.' The people came repenting of their sin whilst being baptised.

Then said Paul, John verily baptised with the baptism of repentance, saying unto the people, that they should believe on Him which should come after me, that is on Christ Jesus.

(Acts 19:4, KJV)

The whole picture that emerges here is that repentant sinners, convicted of their sins by the Holy Spirit, would come to John the Baptist, repenting as they came. Once they had been fully immersed, they had died to their old life, and turned from their old sinful ways. Some say that this was the practise under the old covenant.

The problem with this hypothesis is that the same instructions were given by Peter to the new covenant believers.

Repent and be baptised every one of you in the name of Jesus Christ for the remission of sins, and ye shall receive the gift of the Holy Spirit.

(Acts 2:38, KJV)

There are many people in church today that haven't been baptised as an adult (full immersion.) But the question I want to ask, are they fully saved? Jesus said,

> Go out into all the world, and preach the Gospel to every creature. He that believes and is baptised shall be saved; But he that believes not shall be damned.
>
> (Mk 16:15-16, NKJV)

I would even go one step further and say that satan has brought in this damnable heresy to con people into believing that they are saved. This is just another way to prevent people coming to true salvation in Christ and following His instructions. Jesus said,

> Unless a (man) be born of water and of spirit he cannot enter the Kingdom of God.
>
> (Jn 3:5, KJV)

An infant cannot repent. An infant cannot decide to follow Christ, only an adult can. This is a direct blindness in the Church of England and others. We need to get the fonts out of churches.

BAPTISED IN GALILEE

Whilst Ruth and I were travelling in Israel, we were able to camp by the shore of the Sea of Galilee. We were able to stay there on an official campsite, with all the facilities absolutely free of charge, which we couldn't quite believe when we got there. The manager of the camp said it was free to anyone who was travelling on foot or bicycles, only those with cars had to pay.

You might think, how is this linked to this teaching on baptism? Well, we had been there for about two weeks when we met a very

184

nice, young German couple, Ulrika and Daniel. Ulrika was heavily pregnant, and they were sleeping in their hired vehicle. We made friends and were able to discuss many things; between them their English was very good.

I asked Ulrika if she was a Christian, and she said "Yes, I have the Holy Spirit." I then asked her if she had been baptised, and she said that she had been baptised as an infant. So we did a very long bible study that evening, which went on well into the night, Ulrika translating to her husband Daniel. I said that we needed to go to bed as it was very late, and I suggested that they go and pray, and ask the Lord what He wanted them to do.

Early the next day as I was walking and praying by the shore, watching a beautiful sunrise, I saw Daniel walking over towards me. He greeted me with a smile and a "Good morning," and said, "Mark, I need to get baptised." I was obviously overjoyed by this. Then as we walked up the shore we were met by Ulrika who said, "Well, if he's going to do it, then so am I."

So I baptised the both of them in the Sea of Galilee. It was like a dream. What a privilege to baptise these lovely people where Jesus had walked.

BAPTISING NICK

I thought it best to use two examples. After visiting Germany, heading back to the UK through France, and eventually on to Jersey, we met a man who had asked his vicar to baptise him, and his vicar had refused on the grounds that he had already been sprinkled on as an infant. I said to Nick that I would be willing to baptise him in the sea if he so desired. After he had been baptised, he received the baptism of the Holy Spirit.

One thing to ask yourself at this point is, has any infant ever been filled with the Holy Spirit after being sprinkled on, as promised to all men who repent according to Acts 2?

This type of ignorance by Church of England vicars infuriates me because they are refusing salvation to the very people that desire to be saved, and I fear for them knowing that one day they shall have to stand before God and give an account. I recommend you read the whole of Matthew 23.

I think this scripture says it all, about the state of the Church of England, and others,

> But woe unto you, scribes and Pharisees, hypocrites! For ye shut up the Kingdom of Heaven against men: for ye neither go in yourselves, neither suffer ye them that are entering in to go in.
> Woe unto you scribes and Pharisees, hypocrites! For ye devour widow's houses, and for a pretence make long prayers: Therefore ye shall receive the greater damnation.
> (Matt 23:13-14, KJV)

If you have been led astray by these false teachers, then now is your chance to put things right with the Lord. If you repent, and believe the Gospel, and want to be baptised then I recommend that you find a good bible teaching Pentecostal church near you and make your request to be baptised immediately.

Baptism should not be delayed. When my wife and I realised the importance of baptism, we went to our pastor and asked that we be baptised straight away. He said that he had booked to go on holiday that weekend, but could baptise us in the morning before he went.

NO NEED TO WAIT

And the angel of the Lord spoke unto Phillip, saying, Arise, and go toward the south unto the way that goes down from Jerusalem, unto Gaza, which is desert.

And he arose and went: and, behold, a man of Ethiopia, a eunuch of great authority under Candice Queen of the Ethiopians, who had the charge of all her treasure, and had come to Jerusalem for to worship, was returning, and sitting in his chariot reading Isaiah the prophet.

Then the Spirit said unto Philip, Go near, and join thyself to this chariot. And Phillip ran thither to him and heard him reading the prophet Isaiah, and said, Understandest thou what thou readest?

And he said, How can I, except some man should guide me? And he desired Phillip that he would come up and sit with him. The place of the scripture he read was this,

He was led as a sheep to the slaughter,
and like a lamb dumb before his shearers,
so opened he not his mouth:
In his humiliation his judgement was taken away:
and who shall declare his generation?
For his life is taken from the earth.

And the eunuch answered Phillip and said, I ask you, of whom does the prophet speak? Of himself, or of some other man?

Then Phillip opened his mouth, and began at the same scripture and preached unto him Jesus. And as they went on their way, they came unto a certain water: and the eunuch said,

See, here is water; what does hinder me to be baptised? And Phillip said, If thou believest with all thine heart, you may. And he answered and said I believe that Jesus Christ is the son of God.

And he commanded the chariot to stand still: and they went
down both into the water, both Phillip and the eunuch;
and he baptised him.

And when they had come up out of the water, the Spirit of
the Lord caught away Phillip that the eunuch saw him no more,
and he went on his way rejoicing.

(Acts 8:26-39, KJV)

Here again we see that the eunuch came up out of the water,
showing that he was immersed, and there was no delay to be
baptised, and he was not an infant.

I was brought up as a catholic, and believed without ever
questioning, that what I had been taught was true. It was only
through the revelation of the Holy Spirit and by studying the bible
for myself that I found out the truth. Jesus said, "I am the way, the
life and the truth." You shall know the truth, and the truth shall set
you free.

If you are a believer and have repented, then you need to get
baptised by full immersion without delay.

HONOUR YOUR FATHER AND YOUR MOTHER

I believe that another barrier to healing and blessings is the failure to honour your father or your mother. I would like to share a personal testimony about what I have learned about this subject. First and foremost, God gave this commandment, not as a request but as a command to be fulfilled by man and women.

> Honour thy father and mother that thy days may be long upon the earth that the Lord thy God gives thee.
>
> (Ex 20:12, KJV)

> For God commanded, saying, Honour thy father and thy mother: and, He that curses father or mother, let him die the death.
>
> (Matt 15:4, KJV)

There is therefore a blessing for those who honour their father and their mother, and a distinct danger in cursing either parent. I realised that I could not honour God and dishonour my Dad.

The Lord impressed on me many years ago just how imperative it was to honour my father. I struggled with this, but didn't realise the impact that it was having on me, and that my unwillingness to honour him was a barrier to receiving God's blessings and inner healing.

You see, God didn't say, if you have the best parents in the world, to honour them. In fact, He didn't put a condition with this

189

commandment at all. Some people have had fathers that abuse them, got drunk and beat their mothers, and so on. But God still commands us to honour them.

MY PERSONAL TESTIMONY

When I was a small child, my dad would hit my mother when he was drunk. I often heard them arguing, and I heard my mother's screams. I was terrified of him when he got drunk, but when he was sober he was ok. My dad had a horrible upbringing, and was so badly beaten in with a leather belt when he was a child that it had left scars on his back.

These experiences left me with a deep fear of man that stayed with me throughout my childhood. I developed a nervous speech impediment, and was gripped by fear and a deep insecurity which had a profound effect on every aspect of daily life.

My dad had been brought up in the 1930's and had to become a very hard man to survive. He had served in the navy on an aircraft carrier in the war, and was locked in the gunroom, forced to load the shells. For a man with claustrophobia, this must have been a horrific ordeal. This was before the recognition of post-traumatic stress disorder.

My dad was very heavy handed, and didn't suffer fools gladly. He had been abused himself as a child, and therefore became an abuser. I have no doubt that there are millions of people out there who have experienced abuse by their fathers, and worse, and the pattern goes on.

Despite all this, I still loved my dad, and he was under a lot of pressure to provide for a family of nine. He worked seven days a week, and provided amazingly for his family, and took us on many holidays. He was my dad, and I loved him deeply.

However, as a result of years of constant put downs and physical abuse, I had hardened my heart towards my dad after what he had done to my mother, and the way that he had treated other members of the family.

It wasn't until the Lord showed me how imperative it was to honour my father, that I realised how my own attitude was having such a negative effect on my spiritual wellbeing, as ultimately I was in disobedience to God by not obeying His commandment.

About five years after I had been saved and filled with the Holy Spirit, the Lord spoke to me one day and asked me, "Do you honour your father?" I knew by the question that I didn't, and this issue wasn't just going to go away.

God knew that it had been such a destructive influence on my walk as a Christian that had only resulted in suffering. The Lord spoke again, and gave me clear instructions. "Go and see your dad, right now, and tell him that you forgive him, and show that you honour him as your father."

I knew this had been a stumbling block to me for many years, and I couldn't put it off any longer. I dropped everything. To be honest, I thought, *here we go again*. I wasn't exactly looking forward to it.
This was the second time that the Lord had given me instructions, telling me to go and see my dad. The funny thing is, both times my dad was at home, as if he had been expecting me. Isn't God amazing? He knows everything.

I turned up at my dad's apartment. He was in his eighties, and always welcomed me when I visited, and made me cup of tea and was happy to chat.

To demonstrate that I honoured him, the Lord told me to ask my dad for his blessing. The Lord had taught me the importance of the fathers blessing recorded in the story of Isaac and Jacob found in Genesis 27. I hadn't realised how imperative it was for a father to bless his son or daughter.

My dad had cursed me unwittingly when I was growing up, often ridiculing me, and putting me down by saying that I was an idiot and I was stupid. Consequently I grew up believing what my dad had told me, that I was in fact stupid, and doomed to fail at everything I did in life. And that is exactly what happened.

I was a failure at school; I had a speech impediment and got embarrassed around people. I started an engineering apprentice but I didn't finish it. I somehow could only get so far, and then fail. I went on to learn karatc, to build up my self esteem, and although I seemed to have a natural ability, again in this I failed.

For instance, our club entered a national competition. We were in the team event, but because I didn't believe that I could win, I failed before I started. I had the ability but no self belief. I recall winning the first point, and getting a perfect score, but after that I went on to lose again, and this was the pattern throughout my life.

On that day that I was in his apartment, I asked him, "You probably won't understand this dad, but I'd like you to bless me. I can't explain it, but it's very important to me." At that point, my dad became upset and stormed out of the room saying "I can't bless anybody."

I sat praying, asking my Heavenly Father what to do next, and waited. After a few minutes, my dad calmed down. It hadn't been my intention to upset him in anyway, but he finally sat down and said quickly, "I bless you."

I replied and said, "No dad. If you don't mean what you're saying then it's worthless." He thought about it for a while, then raised his hand towards me and said with great sincerity, "I bless you."

This brought a big sense of relief to me. My dad probably didn't realise the implications of what he had done. But from there on in, my life began to change for the better. I believe the blessing from my dad broke this curse over me.

Although I didn't feel that anything had changed immediately, my own attitude began to change in myself. I realised that all my life I had been a slave, trying to prove to my dad that I wasn't a failure. But now, the hamster had got off the wheel, free at last.

I was learning that I couldn't honour my Heavenly Father, if I didn't honour my earthly one. Even after years of being a Christian, I hadn't fully realised just how serious it was, not only to forgive, but also to honour my dad as well.

We cannot be free and live a joyful, Spirit filled life, whilst disobeying God's commandments. The first fruit of the Holy Spirit is love, and the Ten Commandments are all based on love. For instance, I will not steal from my neighbour if I love him, and so on. Jesus summed up the whole law with these words.

> You shall love the Lord your God with all your heart, and
> with all your soul, and with all your strength, and with all your

mind; and your neighbour as yourself.

(Lk 10:27, NKJV)

The same would apply with the mother and son, and mother and daughter relationship. I know that this had been a huge hindrance in my walk with God, and I was totally delivered from resenting, and even hating my dad, when I not only forgave him, but decided to honour him as my dad, warts and all.

Eventually the Lord softened my heart enough to be able to, not only honour him, but to love him as well. My dad wasn't able to love me as a father should, because he didn't know what love was. Although my dad got drunk and did things that he was ashamed of, I realise now that he must have been deeply insecure.

I realise now that the only failures in this life are the ones who reject Jesus and His loving sacrifice for them. And this I know, that whatever we have missed out on in this life will be unimaginably multiplied in the life to come.

OCCULT INVOLVEMENT

Witchcraft and involvement in the occult on any level is a barrier to receiving healing from God. Sickness, affliction and disease can be the manifestation of a curse that occult involvement, including witchcraft, has opened a door to.

A curse can be brought on the whole family through just one member's involvement with the occult, often a parent, and will remain until it is broken through repentance, renouncement, and forgiveness through Christ. Through ignorance, many are living with the consequences of a curse, through which the devil has been given a legal right of entry.

Obviously, not all sickness is the result of being under a curse, and the good news is that Christ brought the cure for any sickness and curse, and has made a way for all who come to Him to be totally restored.

> Christ has redeemed us from the curse of the law, being made a curse for us. For it is written, cursed is everyone that hangs on a tree.
>
> (Gal 3:13, KJV)

God, through His word, strictly forbids any form of occult practises, and including communication with the dead, predicting the future and false prophesying.

> You shall not eat anything with blood: neither shall ye use enchantment, nor observe times.

(Lev 19:2, KJV)

Regard not them that have familiar spirits, neither seek after wizards, to be defiled by them: I am the Lord your God.

(Lev 19:31, KJV)

People dabble with the occult, many not realising the dire consequences of their actions. If you have dabbled in any of the practises listed below, then you may be under a curse.

A. Fortune-telling
B. Ouiji board
C. Horoscopes
D. Superstition
E. Rock music
F. Drugs
G. Spiritism
H. Witchcraft
I. Druidry
J. Divination
K. Necromancy
L. Freemasonry and Orange order (Exodus 23:32)
N. False religion system
M. Royal Arch Degree-The god Jabulon
(*Ja*=Jehovah, *bul*=Baal, *on*=Osiris)

EFFECTS OF A CURSE OVER A FAMILY:

A. Mental and emotional breakdown
B. Repeated and chronic sickness (especially hereditary)
C. Repeated miscarriages, or female problems, bareness
D. Break down of family and family alienation
E. Continuing financial insufficiency
F. Accident prone
G. Suicides or unnatural deaths

EVIL SPIRITS ASSOCIATED WITH SICKNESS

Not every sickness is a result of a demon or spirit, but there are many cases where spirits are the direct cause of infirmities and illness.

> Now when the sun was setting, all they that had any sick with divers diseases brought them unto Him; And He laid His hands on every one of them, and healed them.
> And devils also came out of many, crying out, and saying Thou art the Christ the Son of God.
>
> (Lk 4:40-41, KJV)

When Jesus prayed for the sick, a lot of the times He healed people by casting out demons. If the demon was the cause of the physical problem, the physical problem will often go away when the demons leave. The bible makes it very clear that demons can cause many different types of health problems most of the time.

The bible does not call the demons who cause sickness, spirits of infirmity; it just calls them demons. The bible calls the demon by the name of the sickness it causes, such as deaf and mute spirit in Mark 9:17-25. The bible does not use the term spirit of infirmity very often. The only time we find the words spirit of infirmity in the bible is in Luke 13:11-16.

All spirits tremble at the name of Jesus and have no choice in the matter when commanded to leave through the power in Jesus' name.

A. Spirits of infirmity, crippling and pain
B. Curvature of the spine
C. Spirit of death (morbidity, looking on the dark side of things.)

OCCULT INVOLVEMENT PRAYER OF REPENTANCE

Father God, I come to You in Jesus' name, knowing that I have sinned against You, and You alone.

Lord, if I, or any member of my family, have been involved in any form of the occult, I confess it as sin and renounce it.

I ask You to forgive me and I commit myself now that I will never again be involved in such things.

Forgive me Lord, and ask that you would release from their influence right now,

In Jesus' name, amen.

I shall not die, but live, and declare the works of the Lord.
(Ps118:17, KJV)

OCCULT PRACTISES

There are many people, who through ignorance are involved in occult practices. If you have been involved in any of the practices below then you need deliverance and I recommend visiting your nearest Pentecostal church without delay.

Possible Demonic Entry Points:

EASTERN PRACTICES

Acupuncture

Japanese flower arranging (sun worship)

Karma

Martial arts (Aikido, Judo, Karate, Kung fu, Tae Kwan Do etc)

Reincarnation

Yoga (involves Eastern demon worship

Zodiac signs

Eastern meditation/religious – Gurus, Mantras, Yoga, Temples etc

Jonathan Livingstone Seagull (Reincarnation, Hinduism)

OBJECTS

Abstract art (under hallucinogenic stimulus)

Amulets (tigers claw, sharks tooth, horseshoe over door, mascots, talisman (magic picture)

Ankh (a cross with a ring top used in satanic rites)

Charms and charming for wart removal

Chain letters

Crystals

Idols

Lucky charms or signs of the Zodiac or birthstones

Pagan religious objects, artifacts and relics

Motorskopua (mechanical pendulum for diagnosing illness)

Dowsing or witching for water, minerals, under-ground cables, finding out the sex of unborn child using divining rod, pendulum, twig or planchette

Psychography (use of heart shaped board)

Occult books, eg The Greater World,
>   The 6th & 7th Book of Moses,
>   The Other side, The book of Venus,
>   Pseudo-Christian works of Jacob Lorber,
>   Works by Edgar Cayce, Aleister Crowley,
>   Jean Dixon, Levi Dowling, Arthur Ford
>   Johann Greber, Andrew Jackson Davis,
>   Anton Le Vay, Ruth Montgomery,
>   John Newborough,
>   Eric Von Daniken, Dennis Wheatley.

Pendulum diagnosis

Hallucinogenic drugs (cocaine, heroin, marijuana, sniffing glue etc)

FORTUNE TELLING

Astrology

Birth signs

Cartomancy (using playing cards)

Chinese astrology

Crystal ball gazing

Divining rod or twig or pendulum

Dream interpretation (as with Edgar Cayce books)

Handwriting analysis (for fortune telling)

Horoscopes

Hydromancy (divination by viewing images in water)

Palmistry

Precognition (foreknowledge of the occurrence of events)

Psychometry (telling fortunes by lifting or holding object belonging to the enquirer)

Stichomancy (fortune telling from random reference to books)

Star signs

Rhabdomancy (casting sticks into the air for interpreting omens)

Tarot cards (22 picture cards for fortune telling)

Tea-leaf reading

Numerical symbolism

Numerology

Phrenology (divining/analysis from the skull)

Planchette (divining)

MUSIC

Gothic rock music

Hard rock music – Kiss, Led Zeppelin, Rolling Stones

Most non-Christian Heavy metal and hard rock music – Slayer, Behemoth, AC/DC, Guns and Roses

Punk rock music

NECROMANCY
(CONJURING UP SPIRITS OF THE DEAD)

Clairaudience (ability to hear voices and sounds super-normally – spirited voices alleging to be those of dead people giving advice or warnings)

Conjuration (summoning up a spirit by incantation)
Mediums
Seances
Ouija boards
Disembodied spirits
Metaphysics (study of spirit world)
Parapsychology (PS) – especially study of demonic activity

SATANISM AND WITCHCRAFT

Demon worship
Black arts
Black magic (involving hidden powers for bad ends)
Black mass
Stigmata
Sorcery
Spells
White magic (invoking hid-den powers for `good ends')
Coven (a community of witches)
Charming or enchanting (attempts to use spirit power)

Death magic (where the name of the sickness plus a written spell
is cast into coffin or grave)
Dungeons and dragons
Gypsy curses
Enchanting
Levitation
Magic (not sleight of hand but use of supernatural power)
Rebirthing
Pyramidology (mystic powers associated with models of pyramids)
Pagan fetishes

Pagan rites (Voodo, Sing sings, Corroborees, Fire walking, Umbahda, Macumba)

Significant pagan days

Spirit knockings or rappings

Occultic games

Occult letters of protection

Superstitions (self or parents or grandparents)

Omens

OTHERS

Psychic healing

Psychic sight

Self hypnosis

Trances

Hypnosis

Mesmerism

Travel of the soul

Astral travel

Silva Mind Control (SMC – Psychorientology)

Thought transference

Pk (parakineses – control of objects by the power of the mind and will)

Tk (telekineses – objects move around room, instruments play, engines start…)

TM (Transcendental Meditation)

UFO fixation

Gurus

Hex signs (hexagrams)

Incantations

Iridology (eye diagnosis)

Kabbala (Occult Lore)

Mantras

Mental suggestion

Mental telepathy

Mental therapy

Mind control

Mind Dynamics

Mind mediumship

Mind reading

Moon-mancy

Mysticism

Apparitions – occultic

Augury (interpreting omens)

Automatic writing

Blood subscriptions (pacts)

Clairsentience (supernormal sense perception)

Clairvoyance (ability to see objects or events spontaneously or supernormally above their normal range of vision – second sight)

Colour therapy

Concept therapy

E.S.P. (extra sensory perception)

Findhorn Community

> Also, many of those who had practiced magic brought their books together and burned them in the sight of all. And they counted up the value of them, and it totalled fifty thousand pieces of silver.
>
> (Acts 19:19, NKJV)

You shall burn the carved images of their gods with fire; you shall not covet the silver or gold that is on them, nor take it for yourselves, lest you be snared by it; for it is an abomination to the Lord your God.

Nor shall you bring an abomination into your house, lest you be doomed to destruction like it; but you shall utterly detest it and utterly abhor it, for it is an accursed thing.

(Deut7:25&26, KJV)

Now the Spirit expressly says that in latter times some will depart from the faith, giving heed to deceiving spirits and doctrines of demons…

(1 Tim 4:1, KJV)

AFTER REPENTANCE
FILLING THE VOID

> When the unclean spirit is gone out of a man, he walks
> through dry places, seeking rest and finding none. Then he says,
> 'I will return unto my house from where I came out.'
> And when he is come, he finds it empty, swept, and put in
> order.
>
> Then he goes and takes with himself seven other spirits more
> wicked than himself, and they enter and dwell there: and the last
> state of that man is worse that the first.
>
> So shall it also be with this wicked generation.
>
> (Matt 12:43-45, NKJV)

Once you have truly repented, if you're not already saved, then
your house, your body, has been emptied, swept and garnished, but
that void now needs filling with the Holy Spirit.

> And it happened, while Apollos was at Corinth, that Paul,
> having passed through the upper regions, came to Ephesus.
> And finding some disciples he said to them,
> 'Did you receive the Holy Spirit when you believed?'
> So they said to him,
> 'We have not so much as heard whether there is a Holy
> Spirit.' And he said to them, 'Into what then were you baptised?'
> So they said, 'Into John's baptism.'
> Then Paul said, 'John indeed baptised with a baptism of
> repentance, saying to the people that they should believe on
> Him who would come after him, that is, on Christ Jesus.'
> When they heard this, they were baptised in the name of the

Lord Jesus. And when Paul had laid hands on them, the Holy Spirit came upon them, and they spoke with tongues and prophesied.

(Acts 19:1-6, NKJV)

We see here in this chapter, a pattern that is followed for a true believer to receive the Holy Spirit baptism. First, repentance, then water baptism by full immersion, then we see that the Holy Spirit was received when Paul laid his hands on them.

It is God's will that you be filled with the Holy Spirit, and it is an absolute necessity in order for us to live a new life in Christ. It is the Holy Spirit indwelling that makes us a new creation; in fact it is the Spirit of Christ Himself.

Now if anyone does not have the Spirit of Christ, he is not His. And if Christ is in you, the body is dead because of sin, but the Spirit is life because of righteousness.
But if the Spirit of Him who raised up Jesus from the dead dwells in you, He who raised Christ from the dead will also give life to your mortal bodies through His Spirit who dwells in you.

(Rom 8:9-11, NKJV)

For as many as are led by the Spirit of God, these are sons of God. For you did not receive the spirit of bondage again to fear;
But you received the Spirit of adoption by whom we cry, 'Abba, Father.' The Spirit Himself bears witness with our spirit that we are the children of God.

(Rom 8:14-16, NKJV)

We don't always have to receive the Holy Spirit through the laying on of hands; we can receive just by asking.

If you then, being evil, know how to give good gifts unto your children: how much more will your Heavenly Father give the Holy Spirit to them that ask Him?"

(Lk 11:13, NKJV)

So I say to you, ask, and it shall be given to you; seek, and you shall find; knock, and it shall be opened to you. For every one who asks receives, and he who seeks finds, and to him who knocks it will be opened.

(Lk 11:9-10, NKJV)

If a son asks for bread from any father among you, will he give him a stone? Or if he asks for a fish, will he give him a serpent instead of a fish?

(Lk 11:11, NKJV)

How do we receive the Holy Spirit? We ask, then we receive by faith.

That we might receive the promise of the Spirit through faith.

(Gal 3:14, NKJV)

PRAYER OF THANKSGIVING

Father God, I ask that You fill me with Your Holy Spirit.
I thank You and receive Your promised Holy Spirit by faith.
In Jesus' name amen.

THE BIGGEST BARRIER
TO BEING HEALED

Ultimately, because God is in control of all our earthly circumstances, as we can see in the book of Job, satan had to go to God to ask permission to be able to afflict Job, and permission was granted to afflict him, but not to take his life. Because God's ways are higher than our ways, and He knows what is required to bring a person to salvation, the ultimate truth is that God knew that without suffering and brokenness, like Job, many of us would be unable to receive salvation.

Although I'm sure it pains God to see people suffer, because His mercy forever endures, God in His infinite wisdom, is all too aware that there's no other way. I'm sure if there was another way, He would rather us not suffer at all.

God Himself looks upon us as a type of tree. There are many scriptures that speak of men as trees, and God, being the good Gardener wants us to bear much fruit for the Kingdom of God. To be able to do this, He has to cut the tree right back, and although the tree looks fairly bare when this is done, and will not produce anything for a while, eventually that tree will grow stronger and will produce a lot more quality fruit.

Jesus said,
> A good tree cannot bring forth evil fruit, neither can a corrupt tree bring forth good fruit. Every tree that bringeth not forth good fruit is hewn down and cast into the fire.

Wherefore by their fruits ye shall know them.

(Matt 7:18, KJV)

What is fruit in us? The first fruit of the Spirit is love. God in His infinite wisdom sees a Christian who may be involved with many church activities, and there is nothing wrong with this, but maybe that person is not baring the fruit of love. The good Gardener cuts that tree back, and one of the ways is by allowing a degree of suffering and sickness in our lives.

When we suffer, we draw nearer to the Lord. We pray more, and we seek His face more. We also consider the sufferings of others much more, which in turn increases our compassion on other people. Because self sufficiency is rebellion to walking with God, we have to be pruned which is painful, but the end result is a fruit baring Christian with a greater love and compassion for others.

There are numerous examples of suffering saints in the bible. Saint Paul prayed three times and asked the Lord to remove his thorn in the flesh, and the Lords reply was,

My grace is sufficient for thee, for My strength is made perfect in weakness.

(2 Cor 12:9, KJV)

What was Paul's response to this?

Most gladly therefore will I rather glory in my infirmities, that the power of Christ, may rest upon me. Therefore I take pleasure in infirmities, in reproaches, in necessities, in persecutions, in distresses for Christ's sake, for when I am weak, then am I strong.

(2 Cor 12:9-10, KJV)

In conclusion, nobody wants to suffer sickness, pain etc. And we, in our ignorance would just want to relieve that person, or ourselves, ..but God. Because God is in complete control, and He wants us to learn something so vitally important to our walk with Him, without that suffering we would not have learned patience and total dependence on Him.

Another fruit of the Holy Spirit, which is very much over looked, is in fact long suffering. We learn so much through suffering that it is an integral part of being a Christian.

I can honestly say hand on heart, not that I am glad for any suffering I had to go through, but I would not have the love and compassion on people that I have now had I not experienced what God allowed.

PART 4

ONLY BELIEVE

TRUE REPENTANCE

Satan has deceived the whole world into believing that we are all good people. The Bible states otherwise, that in fact there is none good, no not one.

> As it is written, there is none righteous, no not one. There is none that understands, there is none that seeks after God. They have all turned aside, they have together become unprofitable; there is none that does good, no, not one.
>
> (Rom 3:10-12, NKJV)

I have no doubt that you may have done some good deeds in your life, but this in no way cancels out a life time of sin. The heart is deceitful above all things; it is impossible for us to see how depraved we really are in the sight of a Holy God.

Many modern preachers have failed to preach the true Gospel of salvation and true repentance. They preach a message that would be very unfamiliar to the likes of Saint Peter. The modern message of today goes something like this, "Receive Jesus into your heart and you will be saved."

This, I have no doubt, has made many false converts. There is no contrition of sin, and some don't even mention the need for repentance, not wanting to offend. Jesus Himself offended many by His message of truth. The Gospel itself is an offence unto those that are perishing.

> For the preaching of the cross is to them that perish foolishness; but unto us which are saved,

it is the power of God.

(1 Cor 1:18, KJV)

REPENTANCE, AN EXAMPLE

A good example of the true Gospel was preached by Peter on the day of Pentecost.

> Repent, and let every one of you be baptised in the name of Jesus Christ for the remission of sins, and you shall receive the gift of the Holy Spirit.

(Acts 2:38, NKJV)

Here in this account, we find that Peter is preaching repentance and baptism for the remission of sins. So what is true repentance? Regret and remorse is not repentance. We can all feel regret and remorse for our sins, but that is only the beginning. For example, we can regret what we have done, but we still go on doing the same old thing again and again, and each time we can hate ourselves for doing it.

Regretting what we do, time and time again, will not break this vicious cycle in our life, which I call satan's merry go round. We regret our sinful ways, so we try even harder to overcome sin ourselves, in our own strength. We fall into temptation and end up doing the very thing that we hate.

REPENTANCE IN THOUGHT

What is the answer to my inward conflict? True repentance begins with a change of the mind, and acknowledging that my life is going down the wrong path which leads to destruction. I have to make a decision to do it God's way once and for all, deciding that I am finished with my old life, hating evil and loving God, turning my back on my old sinful ways, surrendering my life fully to Christ and learning from Him.

REPENTANCE IN WORD

We need to acknowledge and declare all known sin that we are aware of to the Lord. A good prayer to pray at this point would be what King David prayed.

> Search me O God, and know my heart, try me and know my thoughts, and see if there be any wicked way in me.
> (Ps 139:23-24, KJV)

Another good example of true repentance is found in Psalm 51,

> Have mercy upon me, O God, according to Your loving kindness: According to the multitudes of Your tender mercies, blot out my transgressions.
> Wash me thoroughly from my iniquity, and cleanse me from my sin. For I acknowledge my transgressions: and my sin is always before me.
> Against You, You only, have I sinned, and done this evil in Your sight: that You might be found just when You speak, and be blameless when You judge.
> Behold, I was brought forth in iniquity; and in sin did my mother conceive me. Behold, You desire truth in the inward parts: and in the hidden part You will make me to know wisdom.
> Purge me with hyssop, and I shall be clean: wash me, and I shall be whiter than snow.
> Make me to hear joy and gladness; that the bones which You have broken may rejoice.

Hide Your face from my sins, and blot out all my iniquities, Create in me a clean heart; O God, and renew a steadfast spirit within me.

(Ps 51:1-10, NKJV)

REPENTANCE IN DEED

John the Baptist said to the people coming to get baptised,

Bring forth therefore fruits worthy of repentance.

(Matt 3:8, KJV)

This is not only referring to the change of heart and mind, but a forsaking of all our sinful ways, and a desire to please God by faith and holiness in sincerity, ceasing to do evil and turning to God, knowing that we are saved only through faith in Christ and not of our, so called, good works and self righteousness.

For by grace are you saved through faith: and that not of yourselves: it is the gift of God, not of works, lest any man should boast.

(Eph 2:8-9, KJV)

Because we are saved through faith, trusting that He hears all sincere prayers of repentance, and sees our willingness to turn from all sin, knowing that He is faithful and true to forgive, we can have confidence that we are cleansed. Repentance is not a one off done deal.

Although we are sealed with the Holy Spirit, we need to, throughout our new walk with God, keep short accounts. One scripture that helped me to overcome is Hebrews 12:4, but we need to understand it in its true context, seen below

220

Wherefore seeing we also are compassed about with so great a cloud of witnesses, let us lay aside every weight, and the sin which does so easily beset us, and let us run with patience the race that is set before us.

Looking unto Jesus the author and finisher of faith;
Who for the joy that was set before Him endured the cross, despising the shame, and sat down at the right hand of the throne of God.

For consider Him that endured such contradiction of sinners against Himself, lest you be wearied and faint in your minds.

You have not yet resisted unto blood, striving against sin.

(Heb 12:1-4 KJV)

BE SPECIFIC

If you're a thief, you could pray, "Lord, from this day I will steal no more." If you're a gambler you could pray, "Lord, from this day I will gamble no more."

You have heard that it was said to those of old,
'You shall not commit adultery'. But I say to you that whoever looks at a woman to lust for her has already committed adultery with her in his heart.

If your right eye causes you to sin, pluck it out and cast it from you: for it is more profitable for you that one of your members perish, than for your whole body to be cast into hell.

And if your right hand causes you to sin, cut it off and cast it from you; for it is more profitable for you that one of your members perish, than for your whole body to be cast into hell.

(Matt 5:27-30, NKJV)

PUTTING THINGS IN ORDER

We find in Luke 19:1-10 a man called Zacchaeus who was willing to pay back four-fold to any one that he had defrauded, and because of this, Jesus declared to him that salvation had come to his house that day.

This is what John the Baptist meant by producing fruit worthy of repentance. If you have defrauded, you can pay back if possible. If you have stolen, you can restore what you have stolen, but knowing these sins have been paid for in full by Christ, you are no longer under condemnation and the wrath of God has turned from you.

> There is therefore now no condemnation to them that are in Christ Jesus, who walk not according to the flesh, but according to the Spirit. For the law of the Spirit of life in Christ Jesus has made me free from the law of sin and death.
>
> (Rom 8:1-2, NKJV)

If your repentance was true, then angels have rejoiced in heaven, and you are now a child of the living God. You have become a new creature and are now in need of adult baptism which can be arranged by your local Pentecostal or Evangelical church.

> Therefore if any man be in Christ he is a new creature, old things are passed away, behold all things are become new.
>
> (2 Cor 5:17, KJV)

If you have repented, welcome to the family of God.

GRACE SO AMAZING

What is the grace of God? We sing "Amazing Grace," and what a brilliant song it is. It was penned by a slave trader who was made rich by his wicked trade in innocent men, women and children. Like most slavers, he regarded slaves as a commodity to be sold, beaten, whipped, and much worse.

But God had mercy on this merciless, evil tyrant, who had made his living from people's abject misery. God saved him, and he wrote "Amazing Grace, how sweet the sound, that saved a wretch like me."

Grace has been described as unmerited favour, and undeserved mercy. But I think the true meaning goes much deeper than this in the heart of God. For example, we all want to encourage our children with gifts and treats for good behaviour. But would you want to give a gift to your son if he had just burned your house down, killed your dog and raped your house keeper? Absolutely not.

You would probably want to disown him, and have him locked up with the key thrown away. You would probably say something like, "And good riddance to bad rubbish." You would never want his name associated with your family name ever again out of shame. You would regard him as dead and forbid his name to ever be mentioned again.

This is the natural human response to such terrible crimes. But thank God, He is not like us, because He makes all things new. His love and compassion has no comparison with mere human love.

And this is perfectly described in the parable of the lost son in Luke 15:11-32, which I would recommend that you read.

The son had wasted his father's substance with riotous living, and when he had spent all his inheritance money, out of sheer desperation he ended up eating the husks that the pigs ate. And when he came to himself, he realised how good life had been with his Father. He had finally come to his senses, and this brought him to repentance, realising that his sins had caused him nothing but misery.

> I will arise and go to my father, and I will say unto him,
> 'Father, I have sinned against heaven, and before thee,
> and I am not worthy to be called your son: make me as one of
> thy hired servants.' And he arose, and came to his father.
>
> (Lk 15:18-19, KJV)

We see here in the next verses the supernatural love of God. He doesn't condemn His son, or even judge him. He just has overwhelming compassion and the desire to be reunited.

> But when he was yet a great way off, his father saw him, and
> had compassion, and ran and fell on his neck, and kissed him.
> And the son said unto him, 'Father, I have sinned against
> heaven, and in your sight, and am no more worthy to be called
> your son.'
> But the father said unto the servants, 'Bring forth the best
> robe, and put it on him; and put a ring on his hand, and shoes
> on his feet:
> And bring here the fatted calf, and kill it; and let us eat, and
> be merry. For this my son was dead, and is alive again; he was
> lost, and was found.' And they began to make merry.
>
> (Lk 15:20-24, KJV)

Many have imagined God to be some sort of a tyrant, who just wants to punish and afflict sinners, but this is not the loving Heavenly Father that we see in this parable. Notice that the father didn't tell the son to go away because he had wasted his inheritance on harlots, drunkenness and debauchery.

Instead he honours him with the best robe in the house, which is symbolic of being clothed with the Holy Spirit, which would enable him to enter the marriage supper of the Lamb. Without this robe of Jesus' righteousness, it would be impossible to enter.

The elder brother in this parable was probably very hungry because he had been working in the field all day, and he could hear the music and dancing in celebration of his brother's homecoming. This brother obviously thought himself to be better that his younger sibling, and his self righteousness and pride prevented him from joining in the party.

> But the elder brother was angry, and would not go in.
> And he answering said unto his father, 'Lo, these many years do
> I serve you, neither transgressed I at any time your
> commandment: and yet you never gave me a kid, that I might
> make merry with my friends.
>
> (Lk 15:29, KJV)

In this verse he says, 'Neither have I transgressed at any time.' This elder son is refusing to admit his own sins. Although the father wants to pour his grace on this elder son, he can't because of his self righteousness. But the father replies,

> 'It was right that we should make merry, and be glad:
> For this thy brother was dead, and is alive again;

And was lost, and is found.'

(Lk 15:32, KJV)

The amazing grace of God is not for those people who are self-righteous and refuse to admit their true condition.

True repentance leads to healing

USING THE LITTLE YOU HAVE

GOD WILL NEVER FAIL TO MULTIPLY THE LITTLE SEED YOU HAVE

Now there cried a certain woman of the wives of the sons of the prophets unto Elisha, saying, 'Thy servant my husband is dead; and thou knows that thy servant did fear the Lord: and the creditor is come to take unto him my two sons to be bondmen.'

And Elisha said unto her, 'What shall I do for thee? Tell me, what hast thou in the house?' And she said, 'Thine handmaiden hath not anything in the house, save a pot of oil.'

Then he said, 'Go, borrow thee vessels abroad of all thy neighbours, even empty vessels; borrow not a few. And when thou art come in, thou shat shut the door upon thee and upon thy sons, and shall pour out into all those vessels, and thou shalt set aside that which is full.

So she went from him, and shut the door upon her and upon her sons, who brought the vessels to her; and she poured out.

And it came to pass, when the vessels were full, that she said unto her son, 'Bring me yet a vessel.' And he said unto her, 'There is not a vessel more.' And the oil stayed.

Then she came and told the man of God, and he said, 'Go, sell the oil, and pay thy debt, and live thou and thy children of the rest.

(2 Kgs 4:1-7, KJV)

The woman was in debt, and in danger of losing her two sons to be sold as slaves. She had no food in the house, and her God-

227

fearing husband had just died. What a fearful, horrible predicament to be in. But God was going to demonstrate His power by using the little that she had to meet the need and show His power to increase.

The little that she had was insufficient to meet the need, until by obedience and faith in action, the oil was multiplied.

DOUBT, THE WEAPON OF SATAN

The devil knows that the smallest amount of faith when put into action will be multiplied by God. So he whispers, "You don't have enough faith to lay hands on that sick person." This is a lie from satan, who knows that a seed is all you need.

"You don't actually believe that God will answer your prayer, do you?" he continues. The antidote to the seed of doubt is the seed of faith in God's word, spoken out.

> My grace is sufficient for you; for My strength is made perfect in weakness.
>
> (2 Cor 12:9, NKJV)

We can be weak in the flesh, but find strength in the Spirit through the spoken word. Speak it out! "Get thee behind me satan!"

When we pray a prayer of faith and believe that we have already received what we have asked for, then it is done. It *has* been accomplished, not *will* be accomplished. The reason our prayers are not answered is not because we don't have enough faith, but because we didn't believe that the faith we had was and is sufficient.

Some people believe that the provision for healing is only for some and not others. But all of God's promises are yea and amen.

Even though the promises are for everybody, not all will believe, and therefore cannot be healed.

If you read the whole of Psalm 103, you will notice that God promises to forgive and to heal them that fear Him, them that are oppressed, them that keep His covenant and listen to His voice. But we know that this was under the law, and we are under grace. We are saved through faith and we are healed through faith, not of works.

> The Lord is not slack concerning His promise, as some men count slackness; but is long suffering toward us, not willing that any should perish, but that all should come to repentance.
>
> (2 Pet 3:9, NKJV)

I hope this book has encouraged you, dear reader, to go and put your little seed of faith into action. God will never fail you.
Be bold, be strong, for the Lord your God is with you.

> I can do all things through Christ who strengthens me.
>
> (Phil 4:13, NKJV)
>
> Having done all, to stand.
>
> (Eph 6:13, NKJV)

FOR HIS GLORY

Over many years I had developed a mastoid growth inside my right ear. Although it was not cancerous, it was growing and had to be removed as it was pressing on the lining of my brain. I had prayed, declared my healing with fasting, renouncing, rebuking, confessing; I did everything that was in the book! However, I eventually became completely deaf in that ear, as the growth had worn away the bone.

As a healing evangelist, I was completely at a loss as to why the Lord had healed so many people through my ministry, but my condition had refused to budge. Why wasn't the Lord healing me? Many of us do not, and cannot see the bigger picture of what the Lord is doing, but we can always rest assured that the Lord's purposes are always for good.

Our flesh usually leads us to lean on our own, very limited understanding, but we are warned,

> Trust in the Lord with all your heart; and lean not on your own understanding, in all your ways acknowledge Him and He shall direct your paths.
>
> (Prov3:5-6, NKJV)

But so many of us fall into the trap; leaning on our own understanding without consulting the Lord. That is why it is important to test all spirits, as Paul said. I questioned why I still had this very debilitating and frustrating condition. Eventually, I had to surrender to the sovereign will of God and trust that He would use this sickness for His glory, and that is exactly what happened.

I had an MRI and CT scan, and eventually I was referred to a surgeon who explained that he would have to remove my entire eardrum to reach the mastoid. At the time, it was quite upsetting to think of losing a part of my body; but I was trusting that the Lord had a plan to bring glory into this situation.

I went into hospital, and the fire of the Holy Spirit began to fall. When I was at my weakest, the Lord's power and might was being manifested. This was to be one of the weakest moments in my life, and I was giving the gospel to the nurses.

The staff were amazing. Whilst being prepared for theatre, the anaesthetist lady was trying to reassure me that everything was going to be fine, and that she was going to look after me. At one stage, I thought the Lord might be taking me home. Although having a little apprehension, having been in the spiritual realm of heaven before, wherever that is, I wasn't worried in the slightest about dying.

My main concern was for my wife Ruth, but I knew that whatever happened, the Lord would take care of her. The staff were wonderful, but they couldn't understand why we both had such peace and joy.

I couldn't get over the fact that, here I was, going down to theatre, and could potentially die, and yet I had such joy. I can't express what amazing peace we can have when we truly trust the Lord in every situation.

However, the devil was trying to put the fear of death into me, which I, in my old unregenerate self, would have been prone to. But I knew that I was the Lord's, and He was and is mine. Whilst the nurses started to inject me with anaesthetic, I thought, *They don't know that the all supreme Ruler is not only with me, but is in me.*

As they put the face mask on me, the nurse asked, "Are you okay Mark?" "Yes," I replied. Then another wave of fear came from the enemy, so I declared the word of the Lord, saying, "The Lord has not given me a spirit of fear, but of power, of love, and a sound mind." Immediately the fear left.

I cannot stress enough the power that is in this declaration, and if we only ever memorized one scripture from the Bible, this is the one to use to defeat the devil's attempts in causing fear to rise. I suggest to you dear reader, that the next time you are fearful, that you declare this scripture, believing and realising that you have the power over the darts of the enemy and the spirit of fear, through faith in His word.

Back to the operating theatre. I thought, *I have to let the nurses know that I'm in safe hands, and they don't have to worry about me.* I could sense their stress levels increase, so I started to tell them that I am a Christian, and that God is with me.

Before I was able to finish my sentence, the anaesthetic kicked in, and I woke five hours later, giving my testimony to a young nurse who was with me in the recovery ward. I was moved two hours later on to another ward where I was with three other men who also had just undergone surgery.

My operation was a great success, I was discharged the following day with instructions to rest and take things easy while my balance readjusted. All the fears suggested by the devil over the surgery had been lies, and a great lesson was learned through this whole event.

The fact is that there are many lying spirits, and the devil had told me prior to surgery, "You're a man of faith, why do you need this operation? How is this going to bring glory to God? Cancel the operation and wait for your miracle. Can God not heal you as He healed others?"

A few days before my operation, I had felt so condemned by this inner voice that I was considering cancelling the surgery. I wasn't aware at that time that for me to undergo this operation was the perfect will of God, and the devil was trying to prevent me from going anywhere near that hospital.

God in His wisdom had strategically placed me in that hospital to reach people who were lost. I was able to pray, lay my hands on the sick men on my ward, and minister the good news of the Gospel to the staff and the patients.

Whilst in hospital, my wife stayed with me at my bedside. I was overcome by the Holy Spirit, who started to break my heart for the people who were in the same ward as I. I felt the Saviour's love for these patients who were suffering. As tears streamed down my face, I felt a deep groaning in my spirit, like my heart was going to burst with an overwhelming desire to see them released from their pain.

The guest house that my wife and I stayed at for four days during my hospital visit was another venue for the Lord to minister to many people. For instance, the owner of the guest house repented and received salvation. She was healed from a tumour in her ear, with instant release from tinnitus, and we were able to baptise her before we left.

I was able to witness to many people who are staying there as guests, including a Muslim man and his wife, a young Indian doctor, and a father and son from India. There were three Born-again Christian agency nurses staying there; you can imagine the conversation at the breakfast table! We were able to pray together for a dear African sister who had been longing to have a child.

I was able to lead a man to the Lord who had been involved in spiritism, and this was all done through the power of the Holy Spirit, which was and is truly amazing. We have since found out that this man has been baptised, praise the Lord. The Lord was able to use me in my weakest condition for His eternal glory.

So the fact is this; if I hadn't have had a mastoid growth in my ear, then people wouldn't have been saved and healed during my hospital stay. It was only after my recovery that I realised that God had used this affliction of mine to reach, heal, deliver and save souls.

Would I do it all over again to snatch one soul out of the fire? Absolutely. Am I a hero? No. Am I ultra brave? No. But I count my suffering as a trophy for God's glory.

I realise at this point that you may be asking why God allows suffering. Let me try and explain. I thank God for the suffering that I experienced before I was saved. I know now, that without it, I wouldn't have cried out to the Lord to save me, and therefore I would still be lost and on the path to destruction and hell.

I am astounded at the incredible lengths the Lord will go to, fuelled by His enormous love for us, to save us. We often look at the cross as an example of His loving sacrifice for us, but fail to understand His incredible passion in going to any length to save a soul.

I was so stubborn and stiff necked that I had to be broken in order to be saved from the wrath to come. Although I didn't appreciate going through a literal hell on earth all those years ago, I can now, and only now, thank the Lord for saving me.

The joy we can experience in this world, once saved, and the incredible everlasting joy and glory to come in paradise for eternity, outweighs any suffering that we experience in this life.

Apostle Paul wrote this amazing truth,

> For I reckon that the sufferings of this present time are not worthy to be compared with the glory which shall be revealed in us.
>
> (Rom 8:18, KJV)

Yes, we all suffer in one way or another in this world. But, one day, Jesus is going to put an end to it all, and there will be a new heaven and a new earth, then all pain and suffering will cease. We will not remember the former things of this life; they will not exist, because the past will be no more. Our future is sealed and paradise is assured for those who belong to Jesus.

Remember, Jesus died to save, heal, and deliver you by His atoning sacrifice on the cross. It was and still is the greatest act of love recorded in the history of this world.

If you have not given your life to Christ, you need to do so, whilst you have today, because none of us know if we will have tomorrow.

> Do not boast about tomorrow, for you do not know what a Day may bring forth.

(Prov 27:1 KJV)

If you have believed, repented, and been baptised, then God, through His word, declares you saved. Welcome to the eternal family of God. Praise and honour and glory to Jesus, God Almighty, who is the coming, conquering King.

THE WAY OF SALVATION

A Poem by Jenny Halligan

Nothing is too big, and nothing is too small
To place into God's hands, He watches over all.
Things may look complicated,
You might feel that that's the case,
And there's nothing we can't face
When He takes us by the hand and leads
Us where we think we cannot go.
It's amazing how we find all things begin to flow
When we're in tune with His Holy Spirit
And we're following his plan.
There is nothing better that will thrill the soul of man!
So, come to Him afresh, come to Him today,
Let nothing of yourself be standing in the way.

Jenny Halligan

23675406R00146

Printed in Poland
by Amazon Fulfillment
Poland Sp. z o.o., Wrocław